A Journey of Learning and Insight

A Journey of Learning and Insight

Chan Master Sheng Yen

Dharma Drum

Dharma Drum Publishing Corp.
New York & Taipei
2012

DHARMA DRUM PUBLISHING CORPORATION

5F, No.186, Gongguan Road
Beitou District, Taipei 11244, Taiwan (R.O.C.)

www.ddc.com.tw

First Edition
Printed in Taiwan, March 2012

A JOURNEY OF LEARNING AND INSIGHT
by Chan Master Sheng Yen

ISBN: 978-957-598-580-6

North America distributor:
Chan Meditation Center
90-56 Corona Ave., Elmhurst, NY 11373
Phone: (718) 592-6593
Fax: (718) 592-0717
www.chancenter.org

Contents

Series Foreword   *vii*

Acknowedgements   *ix*

Author's Preface   *xi*

Chapter 1   Childhood and Youth   *1*

Chapter 2   Life in the Army   *21*

Chapter 3   Becoming a Monk and
              Returning To the Life of a Monk   *47*

Chapter 4   The Vinaya and the Agamas   *57*

Chapter 5   Religion and History   *69*

Chapter 6   Life Studying Abroad   *85*

Chapter 7   Views from Every Aspect of
              Japanese Buddhism   *95*

Chapter 8   My Master's Thesis   *117*

Chapter 9   East and West   *137*

Chapter 10   Traveling and Writing   *155*

Chapter 11   Standing at the Crossroads
              Looking at the Street Scenes   *175*

The Chronicle   *190*

Also by Chan Master Sheng Yen   *192*

Series Foreword

During his long career as a monk, teacher of Buddadharma, and founder of monasteries, meditation centers, and educational institutions, Master Sheng Yen (1930-2009) was also a very prolific lecturer, scholar, and author. Over the years, his published works in many languages have benefited students and seekers of the Dharma all over the world. To continue and further this blessing, Dharma Drum Mountain is committed to a long-term goal of translating selected volumes of the *Complete Works of Master Sheng Yen* from Chinese into English. This current volume, which we are pleased to present, is from this series.

There are more than one hundred volumes of the *Complete Works*. They cover three broad areas: (1) scholarly works, consisting of commentaries on major Mahayana and earlier scriptures, vinaya (monastic discipline), and seminal writings by Chinese Buddhist thinkers and Chan masters; (2) writings on the practice of Chan meditation for people at beginner and advanced levels; and (3) discourses on the practice of Chan in daily life with emphasis on a humanistic perspective.

Founded by Master Sheng Yen, Dharma Drum Mountain is an international organization engaging in three distinct types of academic, Chan practice and humanitarian activities that aim to uplift the character of humanity and create a pure land on earth.

The Complete Works Translation Project, with the support of its Editorial Committee, thanks all who have made possible the publication of this and other volumes in the Series: donors, sponsors, translators, editors, proofreaders, graphic artists, monastic and lay disciples, and volunteers. We hope that this Series will help realize Master Sheng Yen's vision for a better world.

The Editorial Committee:

Dr. Chun-fang Yu (Chair)
Sheng Yen Professor of Chinese Buddhist Studies,
Columbia University

Dr. Daniel B. Stevenson
Associate Professor, University of Kansas

Dr. Jimmy Yu
Sheng Yen Assistant Professor, Florida State University

Complete Works Translation Project

Acknowledgements

The publication of this book, *A Journey of Learning and Insight* (聖嚴 法師學思歷程: *Sheng Yen Fashi Xue Si Li Cheng*) was made possible through the efforts of many people, including the sangha of Dhama Drum Mountain, lay members, and volunteers.

For their specific contributions, we thank the following:

Teacher:	Master Sheng Yen
Series Editor:	Venerable Chang Wu
Translator:	Venerable Chang Luo
Editor:	Ernest Heau
Editorial Assistance:	Jenni Larson

Author's Preface

I am an ordinary Buddhist monk born in 1930 at a village in Jiangsu Province, Nantong County. The second year after my birth, there was a great flooding of the Yangzi River, which washed away our home and everything we owned. We were impoverished. My family then moved to the south bank of the Yangzi River. I was always weak in physique and prone to illness since childhood. I entered school at the age of nine, and left school when I was thirteen. I became a monk when I was fourteen [thirteen according to the Western way of recording age]. The basic education I received was equivalent to that of a fourth grade primary school student. While the other teenagers were studying at high school and university, I was busy working as a young monk and performing ritual services. Later, I served in the military for the country. Nevertheless, since I was young, I realized the importance of knowledge and education. I would take hold of any opportunity for self-study, and read many books. Meeting the educational requirements along with my published work, I was enrolled in Rissho University in Tokyo. Within six years time, I completed both a master's and a doctoral degree in Buddhist Literature.

From the time I realized that the sutras are used to provide knowledge and methods to purify society and the human mind, I felt lament. I thought, "The Dharma is so good, yet so few people know about it, and so many people misunderstand it." Ordinary people treat Buddhadharma as something secular or mystical; at best they treat it as an academic study. Actually, Buddhism is a religion that applies wisdom and compassion to purify the human world.

Thus, I vowed to use contemporary ideas and language to introduce to others the true meaning of the Dharma that was forgotten, and to revive the spirit of Shakyamuni Buddha. As a result, I read a variety of books, especially Buddhist texts, which I studied and later wrote about assiduously.

Since my early years, I started submitting articles for publication, the materials ranging from literature and art to theoretical, from religious to theological, from articles on secular knowledge to academic theses on specific subjects. I have written for over 50 years and published over 40 books including those written in Chinese, Japanese, and English. They were published in Taiwan, Tokyo, the United States, and London, etc. In addition, several of my publications have been translated into Italian, Czech, Vietnamese, and other languages. Buddhism is a religion that emphasizes practice. Through the cultivation of one's mental stability and calmness, one can achieve balance of the body and mind, improve one's character, lessen self-centeredness, care for others, and purify society. As a result, the objective of my personal reading and writing was to clarify and to give guidance on the theoretical concepts and practice methods. Primarily, my works follow the guidelines of placing emphasis on upholding moral precepts, teaching Chan practice, and clarifying concepts. I am personally compelled to follow the path of placing equal weight on the three Buddhist disciplines of precepts, meditation and wisdom. Thus, I would not be limited to the scope of what ordinary people would call Precepts Master, Chan Master or Dharma Master. For myself, I would always assume the status of Dharma Master because it is best to take its meaning of "taking the Dharma as one's master."

Due to the depth and extensiveness of Buddhadharma, one discovers through academic research that it is truly a great treasure in the history of world culture. To enhance the educational level and academic status of Buddhists, I have undertaken endeavors in Buddhist education and Buddhist research. I have been a professor at the Institute of Buddhist Studies of Chinese Culture University and Soochow University. I was invited to teach thesis writing to students in the doctorate program at the graduate school of National Chengchi University. I have also established the Chung-Hwa Institute of Buddhist Studies, which has been accredited by the Ministry of Education, to nourish professional Buddhist academic and educational talents. Beginning in 1990, our institute held the First Chung-Hwa International Conference on Buddhism, hosting it again every two to three years, with Buddhist Traditions and Modern Society as the permanent topic. We gather leading Buddhist scholars worldwide to do research and hold discussions in various professional fields, for the purpose of practical application in today's society.

It is through the opportunity of holding International Conferences on Buddhism that I became associated with the famous Professor Fu Weixun at Temple University. He and his friend Prof. Sandra A. Wawrytko attended our International Conference twice, and gave us many suggestions. After the two conferences, they assisted in compiling both the Chinese and English versions of all the papers. They also helped promote the publishing of our conference papers through Dongda Publishing Corp. and the Greenwood Press, thus allowing the papers to receive attention from academic circles worldwide.

Currently, Prof. Fu Weixun was invited by Zhong Huimin, the chief editor of Cheng Chung Books, to compile the book series, *The Study and Thought of Contemporary Academics (Dangdai xueren xuesi licheng).* I am honored that Prof. Fu selected my writings for submission to represent the Buddhist community and for the religious community to gain identity within academic circles. It is a true honor in my life. When I submitted my manuscript, I left out the preface due to my busy schedule. Now before publishing, in light of the editor's request, I have completed this preface after my trip to Mainland China, passing through Hong Kong, and on my way to America.

Master Sheng Yen
Rio Hotel, Hong Kong,
April 26, 1993

Chapter 1

Childhood and Youth

A Carefree Childhood

I was born in 1930, in Xiaoniang Harbor, near Wolf Hills, Nantong County, Jiangsu Province. I have no memory of my place of birth because in 1931, the great Yangzi River flood washed everything away while I was still an infant. Not only the properties, but also the land along the northern and southern banks of the river was all under water. As far as I can remember, the place where I was born was already under the Yangzi River, at a distance several miles from its banks.

According to my parents, our family, surnamed Chang, originally lived at the Jiaopen Embankment on Chongming Island located at the delta of the mouth of the Yangzi River. From its name, one can tell it should be a swampy area near the sea. Due to a great flood, my great-great-grandfather moved to the Wolf Hills area near Nantong County. When I was born my family and close relatives all lived in the area of Nantong and Haimen. The dialect we used still retained the Chongming accent. After 1931 most of our family moved to Changyinsha of Changshu County, though some distant relatives in Haimen County remained there. Thus, [the dire effects of] the flood as well as the need to relocate deeply affected my family's history and brought tremendous suffering to our family.

Due to generations of moving and loss of home, we lacked the means to raise a large family of three-to-five generations, and we did not have the financial resources to build an ancestral hall. Although I had heard from my father that our family had a genealogy, I have never seen it. My father was illiterate, so he did not pay much attention to that kind of thing. At present, I only know that my grandfather is Chang Xifan, my grandmother's surname is Jiang, and my father is Chang Xuancai, my mother's surname is Chen. Although once there was a *zhuang yuan* (winner of the national civil examinations in the old days) by the name Chang Jizhi who came from our family, as for others, aside from having the surname of Chang, they have no kinship with my family.

After the Yangzi River washed everything away, my family moved to Jiangnan. My parents brought their six children, rented seven acres of land, built three thatched huts, and worked as tenant farmers and day laborers to sustain the family. I remember this during the Japanese invasion: due to the need for strategic [war] materials, in our countryside we planted a single crop of rice, mint, and beans, and then we alternated those crops with cotton each year. No matter what we planted, we never had enough to eat because the crops were used to pay the landlord and for army provisions. I was ten years old, had to work as a child laborer, and was drafted by the army to help build military structures. In this period it was said that "the masses live in dire poverty" and the people must face the misery of struggling to survive. I witnessed it but in the eyes of a child, there are not many worries or uneasiness when you think that life has always been like this. But later, hearing grownups relate and discuss historical events, I came to know that in the era of my birth China faced strong external rivalries, and was also torn by internal strife among the warlords. Most unfortunate was the Japanese invasion, causing overall restlessness and turmoil in Mainland China. That was the unfortunate time I was born in, encountering the chaos of war.

Our family was impoverished, and in our countryside even the wealthy were poor because the whole country was poverty-stricken. Seeing our landlord's courtyard, I could tell they owned more properties, had more land, and had more provisions and clothing, but their quality of life was more or less the same as ours. At the time, it was said that there were three university graduates in Changshu County, and our landlord's son was one of them. Our countryside treated him as a modern *zhuang yuan*. However, in 1948, the landlord's family's fortunes soon deteriorated. To escape the turmoil and dangers of the countryside, and to seek refuge with their relatives in Shanghai, they rode in the same ordinary class railway car as my third eldest brother.

In my memory, there were no intellectuals in our Chang family. The conditions at the time prevented them from being literate and there was no schooling. I have three elder brothers and two elder sisters. Only my second eldest brother was roughly literate due to self-study and the other four were all illiterate. There were no public schools available at the time, only private schools and private tutelage schools. If the parents were to send their children to study, they would endure a double loss: the first being that the school required tuition fees and uniform expenditures, the second, when the children were at school they had no time to do chores at home, and that was a loss of manual labor. For an impoverished family like ours, it was simply unaffordable.

As a child I was feeble and mentally deficient. My body was often prone to illness because it is said that my mother was already 42 when she gave birth to me, and as a poor woman in the countryside, she didn't have any milk to feed me. In addition the food at the time was coarse (poor in quality, lacking in nutrients) and scarce, so I was malnourished. As a child my growth was extremely slow; I did not learn to walk till I was three years old, or talk until I was five. When I was nine, my brothers and sisters had already grown up and helped my parents by earning money, so the family decided to send me to a private tutelage school. In my first class, four lines and twelve words were taught: "*Shang da ren / Kong yi ji / Hua san qian / Qi shi shi.*" However, I didn't know their meaning. The tutor did not explain then that they meant: "The greatest man is Confucius; he taught three thousand students, and seventy became gentlemen." This was the normal style of teaching of private tutelage schools.

I attended a total of four private tutelage schools for two reasons: first, the tutelage teacher's classes didn't survive very long, and second, my family could not consistently afford my tuition fees, so I needed to work to supplement my family's income. I formally entered primary school when I was twelve. I began in the second semester of the third grade and completed fourth grade in the second year. Due to a poor yearly harvest our family was in wretched poverty, so I left school and went with my father and brothers to the Southern Bank of Yangzi River to build a dike for the new reclaimed land, and so I became a child laborer.

Juvenile without Regrets

In 1943, according to the Chinese [method of calculating age], I was already 14 years old. Actually, it wasn't until December of the lunar calendar that year that I would turn thirteen. I left home [to become a monk] both willingly and compelled by conditions. There were no renunciants (people who leave home to join a monastery) in our hometown, and no formal monastery. The religion we encountered was a kind of folk belief with a mixture of buddhas, deities, gods, and ghosts, the kind of social custom that treats Buddhist faith as the same as praying to gods, making offerings to ancestors, and worshiping ghosts. For example, when someone was ill, and the doctors couldn't cure them, the family would pray to the gods, buddhas, deities, or seek help from a children's medium or shamans. Although my old home was originally located at the northern bank of the Yangzi River, not far away from the Guangjiao Monastery of Wolf Mountain, Nantong, I had no knowledge of Buddhist concepts and its essence. Occasionally, when the neighbors or relatives in the countryside were in bereavement, they would invite monks, Taoist priests, *zhaigong* (male practitioners) and *zhaigu* (female practitioners) to recite scriptures and perform repentance ceremonies. This was a local custom known as *zuo daochang* (performing Taoist rites). As a child, it seemed to me that people had been like that since the beginning of time, and I was not able to tell whether this kind of custom was good or bad, proper or not.

However, the summer of that year there was a neighbor, Mr. Dai, who had just come back from his trip to Wolf Mountain in Jiangbei. Passing by our house, he encountered heavy rain and came in for shelter. When he saw me, he remembered that the abbot of Guangjiao Monastery of Wolf Mountain had asked him to seek out a young man from the Jiangnan area [south of the Yangzi] to become a monk. He asked my mother about this, and in a joking manner, she turned to me: "Do you want to become a monk?" I had no thoughts and no idea about what being a monk meant, so I said, "Wonderful! Of course I would!" My mother was dumbfounded but she consented. She gave neighbor Dai my birth date so he could go to the abbot at Wolf Mountain, who would then ask for instructions in front of the

Buddha. That autumn, [after anxious waiting for a positive response from Wolf Mountain Monastery,] Mr. Dai and I traveled across the river and up the mountain [where I was to begin life as a monk].

Within Jiangsu Province, north of Yangzi River, the very north starts from Xuzhou, and the south ends at Chongming. Other than Yuntai Mountain of Lianyun Harbor, just nine miles south of Nantong City, there are five mountains facing the Yangzi River. Their names from right to left [on the map] are Clay Mountain (*Huangni Shan*), Saddle Mountain (*Ma'an Shan*), Wolf Mountain (*Lang Shan*) in the middle, followed by Sword Mountain (*Jian Shan*) and Military Mountain (*Jun Shan*). Among the five mountains, Wolf Mountain is the most majestic, and had been a natural military stronghold since ancient times. It also served as the sacred place for faithful pilgrimages of the people from the Subei district. The information and historical materials concerning Wolf Mountain can be found in two of my books—*The Journey Home* (Chn. *Guicheng*), and *Source of Dharma, Source of Life* (Chn. *Fayuan xueyuan*), which include a number of detailed accounts. The oldest source material, in four chapters, is *The Record of Wolf Mountain of the Five Mountains* (*Langwushan Zhi*) compiled by Fort Commander Wang Yangde in 1616. Currently, only the Library in the Beijing Guangji Monastery has a collection (No.683.21, 8113:1), and it is a copy of the 1935 printed edition from Guangjiao Monastery on Wolf Mountain. When I was at Wolf Mountain, I saw that my grandmaster kept one collection; however, when I returned to Mainland China to visit Guangjiao Monastery in 1988, this collection had already been lost.

The history of Wolf Mountain began during the period of Emperor Gaozu of Tang Dynasty between 661 and 669. There was a Master Sengqie who came from Xiyu (in the western region) to establish a monastery at Wolf Mountain. Then Chan Master Zhihuan, along with the local lay Buddhists, built the Grand Buddha Hall and named it Guangjiao Buddhist Temple. Even today the front Buddha Hall on the mountain has a statue of Master Sengqie, and half way up the mountain there is a tower dedicated to Master Zhihuan. Legend has it that Master Sengqie passed away in 708 and that during his lifetime, he often performed miracles. He once manifested as the Eleven-Faced Guanyin Bodhisattva. This is why the later generations treated him as the incarnation of Guanyin. Emperor Zhongzong of Tang Dynasty honored him as the Imperial Master, so his honorific title after his death was Great Imperial Master Grand Bodhisattva. His statue is in a sitting posture, wearing a Vairochana Buddha ritual crown and dressed in the Emperor's Great Dragon robe of the imperial court. It is rare to see such an example that is not completely secular or monk-like in the *Biographical Collection of Eminent Monks*.

The monastic administration at Wolf Mountain underwent many changes, namely, from being an open-door monastery to a hereditary monastery with seven sects (mutual governance from divided sects). When I arrived at the mountain, it was under the sectarian era. The seven sects took turns each year to jointly manage the Grand Buddha Hall and the Great Saint Hall on the mountaintop. In 1943, it was our sect's turn, the fourth branch of the Dharma Gathering Temple (*Faju An*), to take care of the duties on the mountaintop.

According to Chinese monastic regulations, if the abbot is selected from monks who came from the "ten directions" [that is, not affiliated with that monastery,] then it is known as an open-door monastery. If the tonsure master [who transmits the precepts and shaves the head of disciples] passes on the monastery to his disciples and so on down, then it is called a hereditary monastery. The early monasteries, however, all belonged to the open-door category, which were supported by government funding. Later, there were privately constructed monasteries and liberty in tonsure (not requiring government approval), so the small-scale monasteries developed into hereditary monasteries. Naturally, after being ruled by the state government, and especially after the 10-year Communist Cultural Revolution, Guangjiao Monastery of Wolf Mountain combined the whole mountain into one monastery. Furthermore, all the monks within Nantong district were gathered at Guangjiao Monastery. As a result, it was unlikely that Wolf Mountain would return to being a hereditary monastery any time soon.

My first impressions of Wolf Mountain were of the tall mountains and of the monastery filled with people. Since it was crowded with visitors, the monks were busy too. Because it was a pilgrimage monastery, tending to the incense at each Buddha Hall was an extremely engaging job, especially during the year that it was our turn to take care of the mountaintop. However, in the winter that year in Subei, random gunfights between the Communist New Fourth Army and the Japanese Army often broke out. The areas up and down the mountain all entered into a state of war. During daytime the Japanese Army would climb up the mountain to dig trenches for warfare. At nighttime the New Fourth Army, dressed in civilian clothes, would come to visit. The young gentries [living] near the foot of the mountain often disappeared or were found shot dead. As a result, the donations we received diminished day by day, and by the New Year of 1944, the mountain had become extremely lonesome and quiet.

I stayed at Wolf Mountain until October 1944, and then went to Shanghai [to a temple affiliated with Wolf Mountain, Dasheng]. I returned to Wolf Mountain in the spring of 1946, after which I went to Shanghai for a second time. Afterwards I never went back to Nantong. My stay at Wolf Mountain lasted less than two years. At the time of my final departure, Wolf Mountain was occupied and encamped by the Nationalist Army, with only the troops left, no visitors, only weapons could be seen, and no relics to be found. The monastery doors, windows, tables, and chairs all became the beds and firewood for the army. Aside from a few monks in their sixties and seventies who were unwilling to wander elsewhere, the other monks all left Wolf Mountain. I witnessed the fall of Wolf Mountain from its flourishing to its decline, from its decline to its perishing. From this I became aware of the impermanence of things as taught by the Buddhadharma, and I felt heart-stricken and helpless. Impermanence may cause flourishing to decline, but decline followed by perishing is not necessary. The world's survival depends on humanity, so I am still full of hope in the future of Buddhism.

My understanding and introspection into Buddhism began about half a year after I became a monk. Besides the elder generations—master, grandmaster, great grandmaster, and great-great grandmaster—that came at the right place and time to oversee my homework, they also enlisted two elderly teachers to help me with my studies. One of them taught me *Daily Chan Liturgy* every day, and the other taught me the *Four Books* and the *Five Classics*. The former was of course a monk; the latter had also been a monk at Wolf Mountain, but returned home [to lay life] after he passed the county imperial exam and became a scholar. The two of them were kind and earnest; not only did they teach me how to recite and memorize, but they also explained the content of the lessons. This led me to understand that the sutras were not only for the purpose of reciting to the dead for redeeming lost souls. Actually, they should be spoken to humanity and for us to follow their teachings. The Way of Confucius and Mencius could be used to guide the world, and the principles and methods of Buddhadharma could be used to transcend the world. If the two work together as sides of the same coin, world peace and a pure land on earth could be achieved. It is a shame that at the time, there was a serious shortage of talent among the Buddhist community, but there were many ritual monks who [mainly] performed ceremonies for the dead. Those who could speak the Dharma and guide the masses were extremely rare. The monks at Wolf Mountain more or less had several years of education, and some even became elementary school teachers. However, there was no one who could speak the Dharma, nor was there a venerable (monk) who was revered and respected by the public far and near. I myself had not thought about becoming someone like that. However, I did have an uncontainable wish, and that was to do my best to learn and understand the Dharma and to share it with other people.

Since I had no choice, my course of study was filled with shifts and turns and did not go smoothly. At Wolf Mountain, although I had two teachers, I also had to perform the duties of a young monk: besides the daily morning and evening services, ringing the bell and drum, cleaning the environment, sweeping the courtyard, and cleaning up the kitchen and lavatory. I was even growing vegetables, cooking, washing clothes for the old monks, and disposing the contents of the chamber pot. As a result, during that time, I learned all the skills and means a monk should have. Although it cost me time for studies, in terms of practical living, I learned the concepts and ability to "do everything on my own" and that "all jobs are equal."

I arrived at the Dasheng Temple in Shanghai, which was a purely ritual and ceremonial monastery. Night and day, I would visit lay families to recite sutras, perform repentance ceremonies, conduct offering and sacrificial ceremonies for the dead, and to bestow blessings and long life for the living. There was no time to study and the temple did not have the financial resources to hire a tutor for me. At that time commodity prices were rising, and the income from performing Buddhist rituals did not balance with the expenditures for maintaining the temple and daily needs. This made me think about the strong inter-relationship between the turmoil of the country and society and the stability of the lives of the people. A country and society is made up of people, so if the people's minds are restless, then society will be in chaos. If the society is in chaos then the country will be unstable. For the country to flourish and the people to live in peace, one must start by delivering the minds of humanity. And to deliver the minds of humanity, one must begin with education. This kind of education is not the ordinary lessons taught in school, but an emphasis on Buddhist faith; that is, using the concept of causes and conditions to console and encourage the minds of humanity. One could also say, "To know the past, observe the present consequence. To know the future, observe one's present conduct." So that everyone can abide by the law, do one's duty, do the best of one's share, persevere in effort, do not escape from reality, do not avoid responsibilities, face all problems, and use compassion and wisdom to correct and improve oneself. It is regretful that even though the Buddhadharma is so wonderful, yet because there were no talents to widely teach the Dharma, so very few people knew about it, and very many people misunderstood it, and even more people did not know how to use it to save the world and humanity.

Under such a motivation, for several years I asked my grandmaster many times to allow me to go for further studies. Thus, in the spring of 1947, I ended my small-temple life at the Dasheng, and started my new life as a transfer student at the Buddhist Academy of Jing'an (Quiet Calm) Monastery in Shanghai.

Tracing the history of the development of education by Buddhist monasteries began from the time of the Buddha. Wherever there is a gathering of the sangha, there must be daily classes, that is, discussions and teachings on the precepts and sutras, as well as the practice of meditation. Therefore, every dharma center and every monastery is in fact a school. Especially Nalanda University at the time Master Xuanzang traveled to India to study abroad [during the Tang Dynasty (618-907)]. He saw that it had nine monasteries, eighteen temples, covered an area of forty-eight miles, and was the largest and earliest comprehensive university in world Buddhist history. At the time, there were more than a thousand professors and tens of thousands of students doing research and studies on various sectarians. Sects such as the Yogachara, Madhyamaka, Mantra, Tantra and all sects of the Mahayana Buddhism were taught at the same time.

When Buddhism spread to China, Master Kumarajiva's translation bureau at the West Bright Pavilion (Chn. *Ximing Ge*) and the Free Garden (Chn. *Xiaoyao Yuan*), as well as Master Xuanzang's translation bureau at the Great Compassion Monastery (Chn. *Da Ci'en Si*), gathered both the eminent monks and elites of the time. And during the course of translation of the sutras, classes on various courses were also simultaneously conducted. Until the Song (960-1279) and Ming (1368-1644) dynasties, the monasteries were often the place of academic study for scholars. Even the Academy of Learning for the Confucian school was studying under the same format as Chan Buddhist monastery courses. At the time of the Qing Dynasty (1644-1912), Buddhism began to decline for many reasons.

First, the monastery placed no importance on education; second, the intellectual elite opposed Buddhism, and finally after the upheaval of the Hong-Yang Rebellion of the Taiping Heavenly Kingdom, the Buddhist monasteries in the sixteen provinces of south-eastern China were almost completely devastated and in ruins. As a result, at the time of Emperor Dezong of Qing dynasty, Guangxu Period in 1898, the governor-general of Hu-Guang Provinces, Zhang Zhidong, wrote three chapters of *The Request for Education* (Chn. *Quanxue pian*) to pledge to Emperor Guangxu to adopt Chinese studies as the core and Western studies for application. He also sought to utilize the monastery properties for education purposes, taking away seventy percent of the monastery properties for the use of student dormitories and seventy percent of the monastery possessions for education funding. When the word spread, tens of thousands of Buddhist monasteries and hundreds and thousands of monks in the country were in a panic and a helpless situation. As a result, the abbot of several monasteries turned to the Japanese for help, requesting the Japanese government to negotiate with the Qing Dynasty officials by proposing their own plan for schooling. The first application was from the abbot of Tiantong Monastery in Zhejiang province, he invited the Japanese Soto Sect Buddhist scholar Mizuno Baigyo, and founded the Hunan Sangha Institute (*Hunan Seng Xuetang*) in 1903. Later, in 1906, Master Wenxi founded the Common Sangha Institute (*Putong Seng Xuetang*) at Tianning Temple, Yangzhou. In 1908, the lay Buddhist Mr. Yang Wenhui (1837-1911) founded the Qihuan Jingshe (Skt. *Jetavana Vihara*) at the Nanjing Jinling Sutra Printing Society (*Nanjing Jinling Kejing She*). Although there were only ten or more lay and monk students, they were all prominent talents, such as Master Taixu (1890-1947), Master Zhiguang (d.u.), Master Renshan (d.u.), and the lay students such as Ouyang Jingwu and Mei Guangxi. Due to financial difficulties, it lasted for only two years; however, its effect on the future of Chinese Buddhism after the Republic Year was far and profound.

The so-called Master Taixu style of sangha education and the Consciousness Only school of Ouyang Jingwu contributed to the nurturing of talents among the sangha, and talents for Buddhist studies among the academics. Both of them were simultaneously developed from the system of Yang Wenhui, so some people revered Mr. Yang as the father of modern Chinese Buddhism. In 1947, when I enrolled in the Buddhist Academy of Jing'an Monastery, there were more than forty known Buddhist Academies in the whole country. Some were closed after two or three years. They were unable to maintain the sources for teaching talents and students, and especially the financial resources for sustaining the monasteries.

The Buddhist Academy of Jing'an Monastery was founded in the spring of 1946. At the time, the monastery was undergoing a dispute between two sects—the hereditary disciples and the monks from the ten directions. It turned out that the monks from the ten directions gained dominance, and they were determined to reform and reorganize education, winning the sympathy of public opinion. The teachers of this academy belonged to the second generation of Master Taixu.

At the time, the education level of the students in almost every Buddhist academy was unevenly distributed. The oldest students were thirty years old and some, like me, were only seventeen. Some students had been primary school teachers and some, like me, had only a fourth-grade primary school education level. The courses ranged from high school to university level. Math and English classes were junior high to high school level. Chinese classes were high school level, and Buddhist classes were university level. For example, the *Awakening of Mahayana Faith* (Chn. *Dasheng qixin lun*), *Sutra of the Bodhisattva Precepts of Brahma Net* (Chn. *Fanwang pusajie jing*), *Indian Buddhism History*, *Outline of the Eight Schools* (Chn. *Bazong gangyao*), *Verses Delineating the Eight Consciousnesses* (Chn. *Bashi guiju song*), etc. The Buddhism courses were all university level, and the Buddhist studies teachers also included university professors, so it was unclear what level we really belonged to.

Regarding these courses, other than Chinese, English and math, I didn't really understand them. When I was at Wolf Mountain, I learned Buddhadharma from the sutras and from chanting, and it was easier to understand. Now, the theoretical and rational shastras were commentaries written by philosophical masters after they developed their own understanding, organization, and elaboration. And there were many shastras with Sanskrit translations and particular Buddhist terms, so it is very difficult to fully comprehend them in a short period of time. As a result, in the first two to three months I thought about quitting school almost everyday. I wished I could understand sutras and comprehend Buddhadharma but after entering the Buddhist academy, I felt powerless and frustrated and didn't know where to begin. At the time, no one told us that Mahayana Buddhism in India had three systems: Yogachara, Madhyamaka, and Tathagatagarbha, and that *Verses Delineating the Eight Consciousnesses* (Chn. *Bashi guiju song*) belonged to the Yogachara system, and the *Awakening of Mahayana Faith* (Chn. *Dasheng qixin lun*) belonged to the Tathagatagarbha system, and what the differences were between them. The Mahayana Buddhism in China had eight systems: *Vinaya* (Chn. Lu), Consciousness-Only (Chn. Faxiang), Three Treatises

(Chn. Sanlun), Tiantai, Avatamsaka (Chn. Huayan), Pure Land (Chn. Jingtu), Chan, and Esoteric Buddhism (Chn. Mi). What were their differences and similarities? The teachers introduced them separately, and they didn't give a comprehensive comparison. This puzzled me. Why were there so many different views originating from the same Shakyamuni Buddha in India? Of course I believed that they were all true and correct, but which came first, and which was more profound? There should be some kind of explanation and justification! I put my questions to an older student, recognized by others as having deep knowledge, and his answer was: "Don't worry so much! We listen to what the teachers tell us, and then we say the same thing to the others! Otherwise, it would be too much, and you'll get a headache!" This kind of answer demonstrated the learning atmosphere among the Buddhist community at the time, which still lagged in the traditional concept of passing on knowledge from one generation to the next. Aside from a few master level researchers, very few people had a sense of how to conduct comparative research.

So I stayed at the Buddhist Academy of Jing'an Monastery for five consecutive semesters. In the honor roll of every semester exam, I ranked the top fifth or sixth among thirty students. This consoled me and it made me feel very grateful. The students at the Buddhist Academy of Jing'an Monastery also had to perform Buddhist rituals and ceremonies in order to maintain our living expenditures and educational fees. The Buddhist educational foundation I have established is very closely related to my studies at the Buddhist Academy of Jing'an Monastery. Today, I still cherish the memory of life at the Buddhist Academy, and of the teachers and classmates that I once lived with. In the spring of 1988, I went back to Mainland China to visit my relatives. I also visited the Jing'an Monastery that had been restored after having been used as a warehouse by the government. The Main Buddha Hall in which we did our morning and evening services was already destroyed. Most of the teachers from that time already passed away. Only three of them are still alive: Master Benguang, who had been a professor at Jinling University, Master Yumei of Wolf Mountain, as well as Mr. Lin Ziqing, author of *The Chronological Biography of Master Hongyi* (Chn. *Hongyi dashi nianpu*). However, I only met with Master Yumei. Among my classmates, I only met three of them. I was deeply moved to see that everything had changed!

Between the spring and summer of 1949, there were about ten or more classmates and teachers who left Mainland China and came to Taiwan. Included are the already deceased Master Nanting, Master Daoyuan, Master Baisheng, and Miaoran, the current Chairman of Taiwan Zhiguang College of Industry and Commerce, as well as Shoucheng, the previous Director of the Taipei Huayan Buddhist Lotus Society, and Master Renjun, who is currently residing in the United States. Among the classmates who left Mainland China, some are currently residing in a foreign country, some are spreading the Dharma, some have returned to lay life, and some have passed away. One [of these classmates] is Master Liaozhong, who is the current Secretary General of the Chinese Buddhist Association, and is in preparation for founding the Xuanzang Industrial Institute. He has contributed greatly to the Taiwan Buddhist community for the past ten years, and I respect him greatly. He could be viewed as an honor to Jing'an Monastery.

My youth passed away in such wandering and relocation— becoming a monk, performing ritual ceremonies, studying, and being interrupted in schooling. In the summer of 1949 the situation was that of one war ending [the Japanese invasion] with another on the rise [the Communist revolution]. The Nationalist army suffered defeat after defeat, and eventually withdrew from Mainland China and retreated to Taiwan. I reported to the recruitment station for young officers of the 207th Division on May 15, 1949. The second day, I went along with Master Liaozhong, and carried with me some simple luggage and a few sets of monk's robes, shared a pedicab with him, and left the Buddhist Academy to report to the communication corps of the Nationalist army, 207th Division.

People in the ancient times had the great aspiration "to lay down the pen and take up the sword," and here we were, "shedding the robes of monks and putting on the military uniform." However, we were still full of strong hope and faith, believing that after the Nationalist army arrived in Taiwan, after reorganization, they would one day return to Mainland China in the future, and let Buddhism shine again. So I still carried my monk's robes with me. My body had always been feeble and prone to illness, so the classmates who remained at the Buddhist Academy mostly advised me, "Don't be in such a hasty rush! According to your health and physical conditions, perhaps in the army, you would be burdened to death within three months. At that time, what use is it to talk about spreading Buddhadharma, and protecting the country and Buddhism?" Fortunately, when I asked for leave from teacher Mr. Lin Ziqing, he said: "May you grow firm and strong by being tested in an era such as this!" And under such a belief, I have been growing strong until now. I am very grateful for his words of encouragement.

At the time, I had just turned twenty, but according to the Western way of calculating age, I was not yet eighteen. From becoming a monk at fourteen and joining the army at twenty, to me, these short five and a half years lasted as if they were half a century. From being a country boy who knows nothing, transformed into a young monk, then transformed again to become a young soldier, I experienced much, learned much, and have grown much. To me, that time of my life was both the years of worries and the first golden era. It is worth memorizing, remembering, and cherishing, so it is "toil without complaint" and "pain with no regret."

Chapter 2

Life in the Army

I Am Still a Monk

Why did I choose the Communication Corps when I enlisted? It was at the suggestion of several officers at the recruitment station. Consider a monk who prostrates to the Buddha everyday, eats a vegetarian diet, maintains a compassionate mind, advocates freeing captive animals and keeps the precept against killing. Then all of a sudden he joins the army, becomes a soldier with a loaded gun, stays on guard at the front line, goes onto the battlefield; there, he charges and breaks through enemy lines, and when the two armies confront each other, he opens fire at the enemy, or even engages in close combat. Such cruel slaughter is clearly against Buddhist beliefs. However, other than the wealthy who could pay for air tickets and boat fares to flee Mainland China, the situation was that the only other easy way to go to Taiwan was to join the army. I had no followers to support me nor any savings, and no sponsoring or consent from my elder masters. So after careful consideration, the only way for me was to enlist. The officers at the recruitment station said that after enlisting enough people, they would immediately ship us all to Taiwan for recruit training there. When they saw that a few of us were monks, and that it was probably improper for us to engage in combat, they suggested that we apply for defense logistic duties.

So it was that we joined the army and put on uniforms. People still called us monks; the senior officers and fellow soldiers occasionally called us monks. Some did that for fun and others out of caring. To me, being called a monk was a reminder that protected my mind and helped me keep my faith. So I felt very grateful towards those who called us monks. After being promoted and transferred to many different units, I would always take the initiative to proclaim, "I am a monk and will be a monk again!" I did that for ten years until the day I retired from the army. Saying that was quite useful and it saved me many unnecessary troubles and perplexities. Many young colleagues would secretly sneak out in groups to eat, drink, visit prostitutes, and gamble but did not count me in. During holidays I had some personal time to do advanced studies in Buddhism.

Leaving monastic life and joining the army was the second great transition in my life. When I was a country boy entering the monasteries, I had to constantly pay attention and learn everything, wherever I could. At the time I only had one thought in mind, which was to do well what a monk should do. So I had a strong interest in learning. Furthermore, due to my wish to spread the Dharma, I constantly worked hard to improve myself. Now, aside from living a group life as I did in the monasteries, the entire way of thinking, talking, and doing things was different. The monasteries emphasized "spreading the Dharma and delivering sentient beings," "precepts and demeanor," "being pure and sacred." The army, on the other hand, emphasized "protecting the country and the people," "military discipline," and being "fierce and vigorous." It was difficult to adapt, especially with meals. I had not eaten meat for almost six years. My first meal in the army was at the recruitment station in Shanghai. They borrowed the Machilus Warehouse on Datong Road, and although the place was huge, to accommodate a regiment of new soldiers, they packed the place full of people both up and downstairs.

And since there weren't enough lavatories, both outdoors and on the deck of the roof, feces was everywhere. Our dining room was also located in such a place, our rice bowls and dishes placed in the gaps between piles of feces. Although the food was awful, there were still some thin pieces of fatty meat floating on top of the vegetable soup, which almost made me nauseous. It took some effort to swallow and finish one bowl of rice. After every mealtime, even though my stomach was empty, I always felt a kind of indescribable fear. As a result, some people left after staying for one day.

However, like most people, I endured it for the time being, because we heard that in Taiwan, the corps of young soldiers would receive a new type of education and get American-style equipment. We heard that the training camp there was like a garden and that the life of a soldier was like being a student. On May 19, we finally boarded ship at the dock of Shanghai Bund and after a two-day journey we arrived at Kaohsiung, Taiwan. After riding a roofless freight train overnight, we arrived at Xinzhu and stayed in an abandoned glass factory from the Japanese colonial period. But when we arrived, instead of a garden or a school, the living environment was as such: the surrounding area was encircled by a ten-foot bamboo fence, our coming and going was restricted, and the entrance was strictly guarded. We had two meals a day and every meal was brown rice mixed with soy sauce soup. We drank muddy well water, slept on straw-covered brick-laid floor and used straws for cover. Three people shared one cotton-blanket. Luckily, when we first came to Taiwan, it was in the warm early summer. At the time, other than the guarding platoon that held some old Zhongzheng-type rifles and a few high-ranking officers who had pistols, the whole regiment was unarmed. Every day, we had recruit training on the sports field and in the wilderness, under the fierce sun with shaved heads, bare footed, bare-naked except for shorts.

At this stage a few of the classmates were very disappointed and in agony because they couldn't adjust and found life unbearable. It was also because their commanders transferred them out of the Communication Corps and into the Artillery Corps. So in the dead of night when everyone was asleep, they escaped from camp and deserted. We chose the Communication Corps because we wanted to avoid opening gunfire and killing with our hands. However, the state of affairs in the army was very difficult to anticipate, and several of the officers at the recruitment station were already gone.

After the deserters left I considered whether it would be better to leave or to wait, stay, and observe for a while. So it was such that for ten years I stayed in the army, one day after another. This, however, was partly due to my attitude: when I joined the army I wanted to do my share, and was hoping to soon return to Mainland China. It was also because afterwards, I heard the news from several fellow monks who had left the army. It so happened that during that period, circumstances for the monks who left Mainland China for Taiwan were also very difficult. The monasteries in the local province refused to accept them, and the monks who came from the outer provinces couldn't even support themselves. For example, one classmate went to a monastery in Taipei to seek refuge with a certain master. This master allowed him to stay for only one night and provided two meals; otherwise, the master would call the military police to arrest him and return him to camp. The reason being that the monasteries were very afraid of the trouble it could bring them by sheltering a deserter.

Actually, in 1950, it happened that in Taiwan, there was a trend for wide-ranging arrests of monks from China. Even the well-known

Master Cihang (d.u.) and his disciple Master Luhang, who had been a lieutenant general, along with ten or more people were arrested and confined in the detention center. As a result, people admired us monks who remained in the army for being safe and at peace. It appeared that it was better to stay still than to make a hundred moves. In this era of turmoil and chaos of war, the most dangerous place was the safest place.

After several months of group life as a new soldier, I discovered that the 207th Division became just an ordinary unit after arriving at Taiwan; it had been regrouped into the 339th Division. Among the soldiers not many were educated. The commander of the 207th Division in the Northeast [of China], General Dai Pu, had been promoted to commander of the 6th Army. At the time, both the 207th and 339th Divisions belonged to the 6th Army. When he came to Xinzhu to speak to us, he asked anyone who had studied at the university level to raise their hands and stand in front of the platform; about thirty or more people did, and then were taken away. He told us that he wanted to nurture educated youth, so next he asked the high school graduates to raise their hands. This time, everyone wanted to be taken away by the army commander, so many people raised their hands. My five fellow-monks from Jing'an Monastery and I didn't know which level we belonged to. We wanted to raise our hands both times; we lacked the courage to do that, so the army commander didn't take us away. For the high school students who were taken away, they established the Student Military Group, and the students were given the basic training as squad leaders at the racecourse at Beitou, which is the present day Fuxing Gang. As for the university students, some of them applied for the university entrance examination, and some applied for the entrance examination for the

Officer Candidate School. General Dai truly appreciated talent, and the brothers of the army all loved and respected him.

Later, our unit was mobilized to many different places—from Xinzhu to Beitou, from Beitou to Xinzhuang, from Xinzhuang to Danshui. Although they were all located in northern Taiwan, every move out was a march on foot. At the time, we hadn't received any communications equipment such as wireless transmitters, telephones, wires etc. We only carried our personal luggage and some simple clothes. However, another classmate and I from Jing'an Monastery carried more burden than the others. I had given my robes to classmates who left camp, but I still carried from Shanghai ten or more books which I treasured and couldn't part with. After settling at a place, the two of us became a "library," and everyone would come to us to borrow books. But once the army decamped and moved on, the borrowers returned the books. So our luggage was particularly large and heavier. My classmate got angry after the second move and threw away all his books. Since nobody wanted to share the burden of carrying the books, he didn't want to share the benefit of reading them. On the other hand, I took my books with me until I arrived at Jinshan Village, Taipei County. In June 1950, I was promoted to Sergeant First Class Radio Operator and when the army was on the move, I had the privilege of entrusting the books to the military trucks to transport them for me.

How did I become a Sergeant First Class Radio Operator within one year after enlisting as a Private First Class? When the unit arrived at Beitou and camped at the Old Beitou Elementary School, a young officer came in contact with us monk-soldiers, and discovered from our behavior, speech, and language that we should all be university students. He felt strange about this and asked us why the army commander didn't take us away for further education. I said: "We are monks, graduated from the Buddhist Academy. We didn't receive high school training, so of course we wouldn't know what university is about!" The officer immediately encouraged us: "No matter what, if the Buddhist Academy isn't a university, it should at least be a high school! If you don't go to university or Officer Candidate School, you should at least be in the Student Military Group. The country needs talents, and outstanding young people like you should go and receive officer education!" So we really did apply for the entrance exam. They didn't test us on Buddhist studies, Chinese, or history; the examination sheet only contained three types of questions—on trigonometry, geometry, and algebra. This is the best way to test for a formal high school level. The result was that only one of us was accepted because he had studied two years of high school at Nanjing Qixia Mountain. The rest of us, including myself, handed in blank examination papers. It was such a humiliation. Luckily the proctor didn't criticize us and instead consoled us: "You are still young, there are many days yet to come, go back and study harder, and come back again next year!" The other proctor thought we handed in blank examination papers on purpose fearing that the officer training may be too strict and harsh. However, by mid-October of the same year, I had already prepared for several months for the junior high school level courses, and passed the exam for the Education of Infantry Squad Leader. By mid-December, I completed a transfer exam for the 6th Army Military Department radio operator training class. At that time, I was probably at the high school level.

It may sound strange that without studying at any formal high school, I could progress so quickly within several months. Actually, it was quite simple. I applied for the exam three times, and each time

I would memorize most of the exam questions. I would then discuss them with the other classmates who failed the exam, so we could help each other. I also asked the classmates who passed the exam on how to grasp the scope and principle of the exam. I passed the exam by taking such a "short cut." Was I really at the high school level? I wouldn't believe so; I was simply accepted out of pure luck.

Because I was a monk from the Buddhist Academy [without high school education] every time I entered the exam, I would encounter difficulties. In addition, my physical condition, weight, and height were out of proportion. My height was 172 cm (5' 8") and I never weighed over 52 kg. (126 lbs.). I once applied for the examination for the Officer Candidate School but I wasn't accepted. Then I applied for the examination for Military Signal Corps School, and was almost rejected. Even at the written exams, I almost failed every time, or was at the border of failing. However, I had faith that no matter which school or training institute, I wasn't afraid of failing, I only feared not trying. I could only worry about not being accepted, not about being unable to graduate. After persevering, I would surely achieve my wish. It was not a problem if my level was insufficient, I could catch up by doubling my efforts. That was my belief. From entering the Buddhist Academy to studying at all kinds of training schools, and even to taking the Master's Program at Rissho University (Tokyo, 1969), I always held such a belief in accomplishing my goals.

Joining the Army yet Not Giving Up Writing

According to the *History of the Later Han Dynasty: A Biography on Ban Chao* (Chn. *Houhan shu: Banchao zhuan*), Ban Chao [a distinguished general from the Han Dynasty (206 BCE-220 CE)], supported his poor family by transcribing documents for the government day after day, year after year. Feeling tired and bored he threw down the pen and said: "A great man has no other plan but to follow the footsteps of Fu Jiezi and Zhang Qian, achieving glorious deeds in foreign wars, and earning the status of nobility. How can I waste my life on writing?" Due to this allusion, later generations would refer to giving up writing and joining the army as "casting aside the pen to join the army." Actually, many famous generals in history also had outstanding literary talents. These scholar-generals who fought in the saddle and wrote off the saddle—a general outside the imperial court, a prime minister inside the court—were called "possessed with literary and military talents" and "both brave and wise." So it seems that being a soldier doesn't necessarily require putting down the pen.

I was a monk, not a warrior, but since I was in the army you could say that I was a soldier. Nevertheless, I was always preparing to return to the identity and appearance of a monk. The books I brought to Taiwan were mostly Buddhist texts and some others on literature and philosophy. There was also a thick diary among them. Everyday no matter how busy I was, I would read a few pages from the books and write a few lines. Especially on weekends when it was raining and we couldn't go for field training, my colleagues slept or found entertainment at snack bars, small restaurants, and small theaters. They did so to balance the nervousness of life in the army with the dull and boring life in the barracks. Some officers even urged that, "sleep is more important than nutrition," suggesting that the soldiers should sleep as much as they wanted to the weekend. This would also keep them out of trouble and save them some money. In a way, reducing the frequency of going out also protected the safety of the soldiers and the army. I should be the kind of soldier most liked by the senior officers since I used my spare time reading. Other than group training and track and field training, which didn't allow for personal time, there was a lot of free time so I read a lot. And when the army was stationed on guard, there was even more personal time. After lights-out I could go to the kitchen, ask the cook for some peanut oil, pour it into an inkbottle, drill a hole in the cap, and use a strip of rag as a wick. I would then find a corner where I would not interrupt other people's sleep, light my lamp and read. Although not allowed by military discipline, my actions were mostly tolerated by the senior officers who would turn a blind eye.

In June 1950, I was transferred from Sergeant First Class Radio Operator of the Army Military Department, Radio Operator Squadron, to the 1016th Regiment headquarters of 339th Division on the coast of Jinshan Village, Taipei County. I lived in Jinshan, Shimen, and Small Keelung for two years more. In October 1952, because the army reorganized, I was transferred to the 6th Army headquarters at Martyrs' Shrine at Yuanshan, Taipei. In June 1953, I was transferred to Yangmei, Taoyuan County. In December of the same year, I passed the exam for Lianqin Signal Corps School at Yuanshan, Yilan. In June 1954, the 6th Army regrouped into the 2nd Army. I was transferred to the Jianjun military camp, the 2nd Army Corps headquarters, at Wukuai Tso, Fengshan district, in Kaoshiung County. Finally, from 1949 up to this time, I had been promoted from Private First Class, to Sergeant First Class, to Warrant Officer. It could be said to be a big transformation for me since joining the army. But if I weren't a monk and if I had a formal high school education, with better health, after five years I could have graduated from the Military Officers Academy; and I could have been at least Second Lieutenant, Lieutenant, or even Captain if I were promoted sooner.

During these five years I read many books, mainly Chinese

classics, and also translated Western literary works. I read general and theoretical books—such as I could borrow—on philosophy, politics, law, natural science, and social science. Some were bought from second-hand bookstands, some were borrowed from the public library, either from their mobile library (books transported by trucks to districts, cities, and even beaches) or by going to the library. Reading enriched my ordinary general knowledge as well as contemporary theoretical knowledge.

At this stage, I didn't have any Buddhist texts to read, and had only been to a few native Taiwanese monasteries, like those in Yuanshan and Neihu. The monks and nuns I met almost never read any books and there were no young people. Other than a few old liturgies and repentance texts, no other Buddhist sutras (sermons of the Buddha) or books could be seen. And of course, there weren't any copies of the *Tripitaka* [the "three baskets" of the Buddhist canon: vinaya (precepts), sutras (sermons of the Buddha), abhidharma (analysis/commentary)]. Later, visiting the Fengshan Buddhist Lotus Society, I saw a copy of the *Shurangama Sutra*, which I was able to borrow for a week. Because they only had one copy, they couldn't give it to me. To me, it was like discovering a priceless treasure. The distribution of sutras in Taiwan happened after 1952, when lay Buddhist Qian Zhaoru established the Taiwan Sutra Printing Center (Chn. Taiwan yinjing chu), and lay Buddhist Zhang Shaoqi managed the Jueshi Book Club. However, they had limited funding and not many sutras. The people who would read these Buddhist texts were very scarce, so very few texts were published and distributed. It just so happened that I had several years of spare time to read some non-Buddhist books.

The young men in the army who studied hard did so mostly for their future prospects, preparing for the examination for the Military Officers Academy, or the High-level Examination [for government officials], or the Test for Specialized Personnel, etc. My physical condition disqualified me for the Military Officers Academy, and with no intention of becoming a government employee, I read with no direction or purpose in mind. When the army was stationed on guard at Jinshan Village, an officer in our company had suspicions about me, and he paid special attention to my thoughts. I was called in to talk to him several times. In that era someone in the army initiated the "Be tattooed to show loyalty" movement which spread like wildfire. Some people imitated Yue Fei, a well-known general in Chinese history, and tattooed *jingzhong baoguo* (repay the country with loyalty) on their back. Some tattooed on their chest the Blue Sky with a White Sun emblem of the Kuomintang of China. Some tattooed on their arms "Long live the Three Principles of the People" and "Long live President Jiang." This officer wanted to know what words I would tattoo on myself. My reply was: "Repay the country, protect the people; loyalty is in the heart, not in a tattoo!" He said: "I think you were sent by someone! You say you are a monk but I suspect that was to cover up your true identity." At that time, "monk" was a very terrible label to have.

The next day, while I was in class, this officer inspected my books and personal library and discovered that I had copied a poem "The Verse of Liangzhou," by the great Tang Dynasty poet Wang Han. It was a seven-character quatrain: "How wonderful is the wine in this precious glass. I would like to empty it all while racing on horseback. Please don't laugh at me lying drunk on the battlefield. How many have returned from battles since antiquity?" Since it was a poem with an anti-war tone, similar to "The Prayer for the Dead on the Ancient

Battlefield" by Lee Hua, it made him even more suspicious. Actually, during that time I had read many literary works. Had he looked at my diary more carefully, he would have found that I also copied many poems and songs from the Tang, Song, Five Dynasties (907-960), and even the Yuan Dynasty (1271-1368). I copied them to memorize and appreciate, not thinking about being anti-war or having a war phobia. Luckily, this officer had only joined our company recently, and didn't dare to make quick judgments. So he went to ask the other senior officers and comrades in the company. Of course, I had been with them for a year, especially with the leader of the Wireless Platoon, an officer who graduated from the Department of Electrical Engineering of the National Southwest Associated University. We often kept in touch and talked. He didn't treat me as a subordinate but as a younger brother, especially when he knew that I was a monk. So this dispute, which almost got me killed, was settled in the end. However, due to this label, nobody dared invite me to join and become a member of the Kuomintang, even after many years had passed. You can say this attitude was a kind of tragedy for society at the time.

My greatest gain in the army was to develop writing skills. At the Buddhist Academy the essays I wrote often received awards, and the wall newspaper would post my articles regularly. I also published a few articles in *Student Arena*, a monthly magazine compiled and edited by our classmates. I got into the habit of keeping diaries and took notes while reading. At one time, the senior officers required everyone to keep diaries; the purpose was to provide a way for soldiers to vent their frustrations, and to reflect their personal opinions to the senior officers. But its greatest use was to discover the thoughts of the soldiers through the accumulation of time; it was a kind of measure to prevent spying. So I used the diary to express my opinions. As a result, whether in the army or training institutes, whenever it was time to publish the wall newspapers, the senior officers would name me to be chief editor in charge of selecting , editing, writing, and laying out articles [for posting on the wall]. My calligraphy was poor, but every time we published the wall newspapers, I would be chosen for the job.

When we were stationed at the Jinshan coastline, I read literary books and also tried to write short stories, essays, and new poetry. I often submitted articles to *The Lion* newspaper managed by our 6th Army Military Department. From becoming the official reporter to official writer, this went on for two years. I also submitted to literature and arts magazines in society such as *Modern Youth*. The author's remuneration every month often exceeded a Sergeant First Class's salary, so I was often invited by the colleagues and senior officers to be the "rich fool" (who pays for the bill). Actually, the money was still not enough because I needed to buy books. Although my writing was still immature and I didn't know what my thoughts really were, I would just write what I saw and thought, and what would encourage me or console others. I expressed my work with a sincere heart and faithful pen and dedicated it to the readers. I often encountered a bottleneck in my flow of thoughts and in the helplessness of real life. However, reading and writing helped me dissolve the anguish of reality and open up to inner brightness.

In 1953, I applied for novel writing classes in the China Literature and Arts Correspondence School organized by Dr. Li Chendong. There were six to seven famous writers among the teachers, such as Xie Bingying, Shen Ying, and Zhao Youpei, etc. So I wrote earnestly, including short, medium, and long novels. Of course my life experience, intellect, and observation of reality were not deep enough, and my novel writing skills were not high. I submitted the medium and long novels to the Literature Award panel, hoping to receive a prize without first submitting them to the papers and magazines. You can imagine the outcome—the works were rejected; I lost faith in them, so I burned them. Up until now, I only kept two short novels—one titled "Mother" and the other "Father"—that were published in *Wentan* magazine. This happened in 1956, and they were later included in *Buddhist Culture and Literature*, the collection of my literary works published by the Buddhist Culture Service Center. At the time, Mr. Mu Zhongnan was chief editor of *Wentan* magazine. His quality was good and the other magazines of his time such as *Gusty Wind*, *Gleanings* (Chn. *Shisui*), and *Fluency* (Chn. *Changliu*) were also literary magazines with more or less the same quality. I also wrote many new poems, using many different pen names, and published ten or more of them in the irregularly issued new poetry magazines and several literature magazines. At the present, not one of them is left.

In the spring of 1956, one of my classmates from the Buddhist Academy saw that I was writing poems, novels, and essays like crazy, but not winning any prizes or becoming famous, so he advised me to write articles engaged in logical thinking and reasoning. He was very much into the political thought of the Three Principles of the People and international events at the time, so he suggested that I write some analyses of international events or focus on political philosophy. This gave me the idea to attempt to write philosophical and religious articles. By chance, my immediate supervisor, the chief of a radio station, was a pious Christian. Knowing I was a monk, he still gave me a Holy Bible. For two months I read it very carefully and took many notes. The same year, between summer and autumn,

I saw a book written by a Christian criticizing Buddhism. Because Master Zhuyun wrote a book *The Comparison between Buddhism and Christianity*, this compelled a priest from Hong Kong to write a book to refute him. Reading it, I felt that I could in turn refute the Christian father's arguments. I didn't care how much value the content of the book had or whether the perspectives were fair, but at least I was able to write a debate-style article of up to 40,000 words without stopping.

In the autumn of the same year, I was transferred to the Ministry of National Defense and stationed at Xindian. Afterwards, I began reading the series of *Hu Shi's Works* (Chn. *Hushi wencun*), the Chinese translation of Bertrand Russell's *History of Western Philosophy*, and *Humanity* magazine edited by Mr. Wang Dao of Hong Kong. These are all works rich in thoughts and ideas. Consequently, I also began writing discourses and intellectual articles for the Hong Kong *Humanity* magazine, and several Buddhist magazines in Taiwan such as *Sound of the Sea Tide, Buddhist Youth, Buddhism Today*, and *Human Life*.

Every time I submitted an article, I would receive praise and encouragement from the chief editor. I discussed two types of issues: first, those concerning human life, pointing out the defects, loneliness, desolation, and suffering in life, and advocating hard work, transformation, transcendence, and peacefulness, believing there must be wonderful future prospects to be achieved by humanity as a whole. These articles were included in the previously mentioned *Buddhist Culture and Literature*. Second, issues concerning religion and literature: I wrote two articles on Mr. Hu Shi's religious thoughts. At the same time, I read his *A History of Contemporary Chinese Literature*. In Chapters 9 and 10, the book introduced the topic of translations of Buddhist literature, and I discovered the Buddhist sutras' effect on Chinese literature. This gave me much inspiration and I wrote an article, "Literature and Buddhist Literature," published in *Buddhist Youth*. Using the knowledge I had regarding Chinese and Western literatures, as well as my understanding of Buddhism, I proposed that Buddhists should respect and write literary works. I also suggested that writers take note of their writing skills and through choice of words, clearly depict the concepts of the sutras, and that they should write with compassionate mind. I also appealed to readers to respect literary works, and not to treat them as small tricks. At the time I proposed: "Stand at the Chinese viewpoint, accepting the strengths of Westerners, to express the compassionate Buddha's ideology."

When studying and researching, I also combined these three guidelines: Buddhist, Chinese, and Western. After the article was published, I received responses from two writers from the Buddhist community, and they separately wrote articles to express their different viewpoints. I accepted the challenge and wrote two more articles consecutively: "Further Discussion on Literature and Buddhist Literature," and "The Third Discussion on Literature and Buddhist Literature." In the end both of them became my pen pals, proving the saying, "no discord; no concord." And they were Mr. Zhang Mantau and Mr. Cheng Guanxin, both lay Buddhists.

Whether or not the thoughts expressed in these three articles were mature, my purpose was to advocate Buddhist literature. And till now, I have no regrets about the effort I put into emphasizing the importance of Buddhist literature. It could be said that since I have studied literary works and attempted literary writings, I understood that to write an article, one must first consider who the readers are, their needs, whether they would be able to understand, and whether they would want to read the article. At the least, I would not want readers to feel pressured or burdened to read my articles, and still be able to receive some knowledge and inspiration to the mind. Otherwise, no matter how many good intentions I had, it would still be torture for the readers. I had this little inspirational thought, and so I have been writing continuously until now.

Buddhist Practice and Buddhist Studies

In August 1956, I was transferred to Taipei because I passed the exam for an Intelligence Interception and Collection Unit at the Ministry of National Defense, and I began doing duties at intercepting and collecting wireless communication intelligence. We faced the wireless operators from Mainland China everyday; although the Taiwan Strait separated us, we even knew their gender, name, and age. They didn't know of our existence or perhaps they did know, but they didn't know who we were. In this capacity we provided results to the supervisors according to our own personal diligence, and being a diligent worker I received several awards.

This kind of surveillance is around the clock so we rotated in three shifts: day shift meant the regular working hours; night shift was afternoon till midnight; and the early morning shift was from midnight to eight the next morning. The most unbearable was the early morning shift, especially for me. Every time I did the early morning shift, I wouldn't be able to sleep the next day. So I would take advantage of the time to read, meditate, and recite the Buddha's name.

At this time more Buddhist texts were available, some imported from Hong Kong and some reprinted in Taiwan, such as a commentary on the *Flower Ornament Scripture* (Chn. *Huayan jing;*

Skt. Avatamsaka Sutra), the *Mahaparinirvana Sutra*, the *Lotus Sutra* (*Skt. Saddharmapundarika Sutra*), and the *Diamond Sutra* (*Skt. Vajracchedika Prajnaparamita Sutra*). At the time Master Yinshun (1905-2005) was abbot at the Shandao Temple, and his student Master Yanpei, was teaching at Fuyan Buddhist Institute. I went to Shandao Temple during the weekends and would meet them occasionally. Master Yanpei knew that I liked to read, so he collected all of Master Yinshun's works, as well as his own works and other translations, and made them gifts to me. This opportunity gave me both the time and the books to read.

A Buddhist should not separate practice and studies but should use the concepts and methods of Buddhism as guidance and means for practicing. If one only conducted Buddhist studies [without practicing], one would be an ordinary scholar who can write books to express their opinions, give lectures, provide teaching materials, or even make a living; they may contribute to the discussion and introduction of historical culture, but not feel much impact on their spiritual life or improve their character. The sutras describe this as "talking about food and counting others' treasures"; in other words, it is like reciting a menu yet not enjoying the meals, or counting treasures that belonged to others; both are worthless activities.

On the other hand, ordinary people may have Buddhist faith, recite the Buddha's name, eat a vegetarian diet, meditate, repent, but not care much about Buddhist concepts. They would not know the meanings of dharma with or without outflows, created dharma or uncreated dharma, worldly or world-transcending dharma, socially engaged or world-renouncing; they would not know the differences and similarities between Buddhism and other religions. They appear to be Buddhist but after talking with them, you would discover that they were no different from the followers of other religions who attach themselves to Buddhism, or followers of folk beliefs in gods or in [superstitious] Taoism. This is such a pity!

For this reason, since ancient times, the Masters have emphasized both practice and understanding—that the two were like the wings of a bird, or the two wheels of a bicycle. Understanding without practice would be useless, and practice without understanding would be blind faith. Based on such concepts, I would of course advocate consistency of knowledge and action. Consequently, I also agree with the theory of "unity of knowledge and action" proposed by Wang Yangming. At the time, the whole country used Dr. Sun Yat-sen's theory of "knowing is more difficult than doing" to encourage everyone, which I also accepted. It would be absolutely correct to treat Buddhist practice and Buddhist studies from the perspectives of "acting upon knowing," "knowing upon acting," and "equating knowing and doing." If we required everyone to act after "knowing and realizing thoroughly," then that would be wrong. The reason being, ordinary people are "slow in knowing and realizing." So Confucius said: "The common people can be made to follow orders without understanding why they should." This is also correct. Dr. Sun Yat-sen stated many examples concerning this issue in his book, *Sun Wen Theory*. Even today, I would still use this point to encourage people who do not yet believe in Buddhism, that they need not have a thorough understanding of all the Buddhist concepts before believing in the Buddha and practicing the Dharma. People should start believing in the Buddha and practice while enhancing their knowledge of the Dharma at the same time. Many people thought that after they understood the Dharma, they would wait until they could uphold all the precepts before becoming Buddhists. If that were the case, there would never be a chance for them to become Buddhists.

From 1957 onwards, the publishers of several Buddhist magazines in the Taipei Buddhist community knew that I could write papers, and that I had submitted articles to several literary and philosophical magazines in Taipei and Hong Kong. They were also aware that I wrote a book about Buddhism and Christianity, so they invited me to submit articles. At the time, I was hoping to write about what I encountered, saw, and thought about several Buddhist theories and issues, and to share them with readers in our society. You could say that it has been my long-held aspiration to convey the correct Dharma, and to convert difficult Buddhist concepts into words that are easy to understand and accept, and to provide them to people who wanted the Dharma. As a result, I was really grateful for these few magazines which provided a place for me to publish them. Although these magazines were for subscription, they didn't sell well, so its writers received no remuneration. However, money was not the issue for me. As long as someone could read my article and accept Buddhism as a result, I would feel very satisfied. At the time, I used several pennames; one I used more often was General of Awakening the World. Up until the present, there were still many Buddhists over age fifty who decided to believe in Buddhism and practice the Dharma after reading the articles written by the General of Awakening the World. However, they mostly would not know who that was.

In recent decades, from the behavior of the Buddhists themselves, or from the scholars' understanding of Buddhism and their judgments on its value, Buddhism could be described by several terms: "superstitious," "passive," "non-productive," and "selfish." Actually, the Buddhism founded by Shakyamuni was not like that. The monks of the sangha had something they would and need to do everyday—practicing earnestly without dissociating from society. For example, Shakyamuni set up the rule that bhikshus (monks) must go into society to beg for alms, using this opportunity to spread the concepts and essence of the Dharma, as well as the Buddhist's living guidelines, the five precepts, and the ten virtues. So they were called the "humanistic bhikshus" who would travel and benefit humanity.

Once, when Shakyamuni asked for alms from a farmer, the farmer said, "We farmers cultivate the fields; therefore, we have food to eat. You don't cultivate the fields, so why should you get to eat?" The Buddha replied, "You cultivate the fields and we bhikshus also cultivate the field. You cultivate the muddy fields in the wilderness, and we cultivate the fields of people's minds." The farmer was happy upon hearing this [and gave alms to the Buddha]. When Buddhism spread to China, social customs disdained begging, so the bhikshus could only plant and cultivate their own foods in the mountains of the monasteries. As Chan Master Baizhang (720-814) of the Tang Dynasty said, "On any day that I don't work, I will not eat." This kind of Chan and farm life was not being non-productive.

However, in recent eras the big monasteries relied on rental income from farmlands, and the small monasteries in the countryside and cities depended on donations and fees from repentance ceremonies and money received from social interactions. Even though these monasteries had morning or evening services or meditation, still, they were disconnected from the larger society. This disconnection is why the monasteries were not operated to educate society, and therefore unimportant in the spreading of the Dharma. Since the need to spread the Dharma was not considered necessary, nobody nurtured the talents for teaching the Dharma, or even felt the need to nurture such talents. This resulted in the impression and image of Buddhism as escapist and not beneficial to society, making it appear superstitious and harmful, like a religion that should be abolished and eliminated.

This was why in modern times the lay Buddhist Yang Wenhui, alias Renshan, advocated printing and distributing Buddhist sutras and texts, and establishing institutes to nurture talent for Dharma teaching among monks and laypeople. Mr. Yang's student, Master Taixu, promoted Humanistic Buddhism; in turn, Master Taixu's student Master Yinshun followed his footsteps and proposed Humanized Buddhism. My own Master, Dongchu (1907-1977), founded the monthly magazine *Humanity*. I myself founded the Dharma Drum Mountain in Taiwan, whose purpose is to establish a pure land on earth. These were all done to transmit the wisdom teaching and save the future of Buddhism, which was suspended in thin air. It was also a movement to return to the original essence of the teachings of Shakyamuni Buddha.

Between 1957 and 1960, I focused on these issues and wrote ten or more articles to clarify them. For example, monasteries relied on repentance ceremonies and ritual services as their main source of income. This caused the monks to use the practice of reciting the sutras, repenting, and reciting the Buddha's name as a means for earning their living, thus losing the original meaning of practice. Laypeople who came in contact with the monasteries requested the services of reciting the sutras and performing repentance ceremonies. They also negotiated prices, like how much money for one chapter of the sutra, how much for one set of repentances, how much for a two-hour stay, for a one-day stay, and so on. This caused the sangha—one of the Three Jewels of Buddhism—to lose its respectful dignity and status, and the monks to be treated as carpenters, tailors, and cooks, etc. Since they were treated in the same manner as hired laborers, they were no longer called "masters" but "chiefs." However, over hundreds of years, Buddhism was sustained by reciting sutras and repentance ceremonies, so such rituals indeed have their irreplaceable function.

Regarding this, I wrote an article over ten thousand words, titled "A Discussion of Buddhist Rituals and Repentance Ceremonies and their Pros and Cons," and my conclusion was: "Buddhist rituals were necessary indeed; however, the ideal Buddhist ritual definitely would not be a kind of business, but a guidance on the methods of practice and a guidance on demand. Because the responsibility of the sangha is to actively engage in the teaching and spreading of the Dharma instead of passively relying on the repentance ceremonies to make a living. Each monastery should adopt teaching the Dharma as its main task. With all possibilities, monasteries should rely on the donations [instead of doing business] to survive. If there were no alternatives but to conduct repentance ceremonies, the Buddhist rituals should be a joint practice for both the monks and the donor. When conducting Buddhist rituals, the monks should do so in accordance with the Dharma and with reverence. The donor's family should also participate in the recitation, taking hold of the opportunity to redeem the dead, and sharing the taste of the nectar of the Dharma. At the very minimum, during the Buddhist rituals, there should be a section explaining to the donor about the Dharma and its essence. Only by doing so, could we prevent the sangha from being treated as hired labors paid by the hour, and to not lose the dignity of Buddhist rituals."

In addition, regarding the negative images of Buddhism being seen as passive and not beneficial to the society, I also provided explanations several times. I wrote in the article "Calming the Human Mind and Transcending the Self-Nature": "Secular scholars often attacked Buddhism as selfish and escapist, saying that Buddhism advocated the pursuit of nirvana and transcendence of the three realms, but not contributing oneself to improving the reality of human society... On the surface, it may seem that Buddhism advocates personal liberation and transcendence, which appears to be selfish. However, the fact is that this "selfish" goal is exactly the perfect expression of the spirit of compassion. Selfish in terms of personal liberation, but to achieve personal liberation requires the actions and mindset of compassion and salvation."

In the article "The Ideal Society," I said: "The people with superficial views would consider the Buddhist life as passive because the ultimate goal of practice is to transcend the three realms and leave the world instead of striving to construct a better world. Actually, leaving the world would be the goal of practicing Buddhism, and building a better world is the actual means of Buddhist practice."

I also said: "The teaching of Buddhism is to allow everyone to perform one's own duties, not only 'to do no evil' but also 'to cultivate all goodness.' Any action that would be harmful to sentient beings, a Buddhist would not do. Anything that would benefit the general public, a Buddhist would do accordingly."

Because I had this idea, I agreed with Master Taixu's proposal that "the perfection of humanity is the perfection of the Buddha." I also highly praised the book *The Buddha in the Human Realm* written by Master Yinshun. Buddhadharma should be accomplished in human society and one should gradually improve until one reaches buddhahood. One cannot reject or ignore its human nature and just talk about the level of the bodhisattvas and the buddhas.

Prior to this era, Chinese Buddhism from the end of the Song Dynasty to the end of the Qing Dynasty and in the early Republic, only very few scholars were studying profound Buddhist concepts, and they ignored its practical application in humanity. Generally, the Buddhists could not understand the usefulness and rationality of the Buddhadharma and only rested on the form and facial appearance of the belief. That was due to serious abuses resulting from the inability to attend to both Buddhist practice and Buddhist studies.

Chapter 3

Becoming a Monk and Returning
to the Life of a Monk

Since joining the army in May, 1949, until my discharge in January, 1960, this journey of my life exceeded the number of years I was a monk in my youth. Throughout this time, my identity was that of a solider but in my mind, I was always a monk. So, when I left the service I naturally returned to the Buddhist sangha. To me this was not becoming a monk again, but simply returning to the life of a monk.

I have already described how I first became a monk at Wolf Mountain in Mainland China. And in my autobiography, *The Journey Home*, I described my state of mind and feelings about returning to the life of a monk: "When I was fourteen years old, I wove a beautiful dream about becoming a monk—that the world of Wolf Mountain was as magnificent as a painting, as marvelous as a poem. Because I held to this dream of paintings and poems, when I went to Wolf Mountain, the dream became a gap between being a monk and practicing the Dharma. As a result, due to conditions, I was not able to keep the identity of a monk. Now, I see that the dream may have been mistaken, but the road I took was correct; so after wandering around in a very big circle, I have finally found my way home."

My ten years in the army were not a waste of my life. I contributed my share of serving the country, and I also found many ways to improve myself. It was a painful process of growth, worth remembering and cherishing. In terms of studies, I was no longer the Ah Meng of the Wu Dynasty (222-280) (referring to General Lu Meng in the Three Kingdoms Era (220 BCE-280 BCE), a model of diligent self-improvement). As for practice, I also had some breakthroughs, especially in my twenty-eighth year, when I was able to enter the "gate of Chan." This occurred through compassionate guidance from Master Lingyuan Hongmiao (1902-1988), a disciple of the contemporary master, Xuyun (1840–1959). That experience had a deep impact on my life, and it allowed me to jump out from the web of ensnaring myself. Since then, my life no longer belonged to me. Not to say that I dedicated my life to contributing to our world and all sentient beings, but that I was determined to find ways to work and study for humanity's needs and Buddhism.

I returned to the life of a monk by taking refuge under Tonsure Master Dongchu, who then gave me the Dharma name, Huikong Shengyen. A student of Master Taixu, Dongchu was abbot of the famous Caodong monastery, Jiaoshan Dinghui, in Zhenjiang, Jiangsu Province. Master Dongchu was a 50th-generation Dharma heir in the Caodong school of Dongshan Liangjie (806-869). Dongchu also studied in the school of Linji Yixuan (d. 866) at Changzhou Tianning Monastery, first becoming a monk in the Linji monastery at Putuo Shan. Therefore, he received transmission in both the Linji and Caodong lineages. Being a disciple of Dongchu, I also inherited Dharma transmission in both lineages. This may appear complicated for a monk; however, this was actually quite remarkable—the Dharma originally being one, to divide it into branches is not what a wise man would do.

At this point, I must make another description to retrace the past and account for the future. Besides receiving Dharma transmission in two lineages from Master Dongchu [in 1976], in the spring of 1958 [while still in the army,] I had already established Dharma affiliation with Master Lingyuan. [Then, 20 years later, I encountered Master Lingyuan again, and] at 2 P.M. on December 5, 1978, he formally gave me the Dharma name Zhigang Weirou. He also gave me a book of the Dharma lineage chart, *The Record of Illuminating Stars*. This resulted in my establishing Dharma connections with Gushan Yongquan Monastery, and becoming the 57th-generation Dharma heir in the tradition of Linji.

Editing and Writing

As of January 1, 1960, I was discharged from the army and received the formal Order of Retirement. The date for exchanging my uniform for a robe and having my head ceremonially shaved for the second time was December 1 of lunar calendar 1959. Since I retired from the army for health reasons, I was hoping to recover my body and mind after returning to the sangha. I was also hoping to take time to repent for my recklessness and carelessness in the army over the past ten years, to shake off the winds and dust of the army life, and to delve into and fully enjoy Master Dongchu's collection of Buddhist texts.

At the time, only the Central Library of Taiwan kept a set of *Qishazang*, the only complete set of Buddhist texts in Taiwan, and only the Chung-Hwa Institute of Buddhist Culture was conducting cultural works and publishing books, such as printing the *Taisho Tripitaka*, which was compiled [in Japan] during the Emperor Taisho era (1911-1925). With the first and second edition, this came to a total set of 100 volumes. In 1959, the Institute completed printing 500 of these *Tripitaka* sets; it also completed the printing of the *Zengaku Taisei*, a compilation of Japanese translations of fifty-nine classics of Chan literature. Master Dongchu himself was a scholar of Buddhist history and before he passed away he completed: the *History of Communication between Indian and Chinese Buddhism,* the *History of Communication between Japanese and Chinese Buddhism,* and the *Contemporary History of Chinese Buddhism.* In Taiwan at that time, it was not easy to find a Buddhist monastery with that large a collection of books as the Chung-Hwa Institute of Buddhist Culture.

Master Dongchu continued the will of Master Taixu to spread the Dharma through the use of words, and advocated [what Master Taixu called] Humanistic Buddhism. Commencing May 1949, Dongchu gathered several Buddhist youths with similar goals and began a monthly magazine, *Humanity.* It has survived since then through the efforts of more than ten editors, and when I sought refuge under Master Dongchu, it was just as the chief editor resigned. As a result, I moved from being a writer to *Humanity's* chief editor. Before I went into solitary retreat in the mountains in southern Taiwan, I had served as editor for two years.

During this time my physical health was never well; I experienced weakness, dizziness, tightness, feeble arms, cold feet, low appetite, and stomach problems. It is said that before Shakyamuni Buddha attained perfect enlightenment under the Bodhi Tree, he encountered obstacles from many demonic states, so these small problems that I had were really nothing. Luckily, an elder master referred me to a Chinese doctor for diagnosis, who prescribed two sets of medicine for me. After I took the medicines for six months, my body gradually recovered from barely functioning.

During that time, not many articles were being submitted to *Humanity* by the Buddhist community, and since there was no remuneration for the writers, acquiring articles was very difficult.

I really respected the previous editors for being able to publish the magazine every month on time, an amazing feat. Therefore, I asked Master Dongchu to tell me the secret. His reply was, "What secret? If nobody wrote anything, then do it yourself! If you wrote one article a day, you would have thirty articles each month. Give a different penname for each article and it would be done. The Dharma is so vast and deep, yet the problems of humanity are so many and complicated. You could find great topics everywhere, from what you heard, read, felt, touched, and thought everyday, and there would be an endless supply of articles." So I asked him to submit some articles, and his reply was even cleverer: "For those editors of *Humanity* who couldn't write, I had no choice but to write for them. Now that you have become really good at writing, and since I'm getting old, of course it would be your turn to write."

And so it was that I had to work hard, from the editorial section to the afterword. Fortunately, there were two lay Buddhists who had been submitting articles to *Humanity* on a long-term basis, which helped to share some of the burden. Although their articles were not very long, they were full of philosophical insight and depth but may have been too difficult for ordinary readers. Luckily, the number printed each issue was only around a thousand, and there were always one or two articles that were worth reading. Especially, when occasionally, Master Dongchu gave oral teachings, and I recorded and published them as editorials. These often turned out to be the "heavyweight" pieces in a given issue.

I was inviting people to write, asking and begging for articles. Several magazines inside and outside the Buddhist community were also pressing for the articles that I owed them. Thus, I had to write, edit, and compile articles for *Humanity* as well as deal with pressure from the outside. With such poor health, writing was a painful task. The spaces for editing, publishing, and funding the magazine were all in my office, and the staff, if you add the others, would still be just me. I often went in person from the Old Beitou Train Station to the small printing factory in Wanhua, to deal with the typesetters—just for altering the layout, adding news, or even correcting one or two words. When it was time to publish, even though their attitude was quite nice, I had to go to the printer up to five or six times. That was not so much fun. As far as I knew, the cultural groups within or outside the Buddhist community were mostly in the same boat, and books were still being published one by one, and then sent to the hands of the readers. Therefore, those who are in the circle of [this kind of] cultural work must have this kind of devotion.

During that period, besides editing, writing, and seeing the doctor, I also used the time to read some larger sutras and shastras, [commentaries, usually on sutras]. I finished reading all eighty chapters of the *Flower Ornament (Avatamsaka) Sutra*, all forty chapters of the *Mahaparinirvana Sutra*, and twenty of the one hundred chapters of the *Shastra on the Mahaprajnaparamita Sutra*. Every day, aside from morning service, evening service, and meditation, I also did the Great Compassion Repentance for the length of time to burn one stick of incense.

The Record of Asking for Ordination

In August of the lunar year 1961, I went to receive the Threefold Ordination (shramanera, bhikshu, bodhisattva) of the Great Precepts of the Thousand Buddhas under Master Daoyuan Nengxin (1900-1988). This was to take place at the Haihui Temple in Badu, Keelung. Buddhism refers to the monastery where one receives the precepts as the Repentance Hall [also called the Ordination Hall]. I was originally hoping that I would be able to study the precepts diligently, and do repentance and prostrations to the Buddha. However, on the first day I entered the Ordination Hall, I was selected to be the head of the shramaneras, which is equivalent to the student leader in an ordinary school. I was to provide services to all the new applicants for receiving the precepts. Furthermore, the secretary of the Ordination Hall, Master Zhenhua, wanted to promote me for my talents, so he compassionately recommended me to Master Daoyuan to be in charge of the writing of the *Diary of the Ordination Platform*. Their reasons were first, that I had been a monk since I was young, and should be able to serve the new applicants for receiving the precepts in accordance with the Dharma. Secondly, I had already begun writing, and had been a writer and editor in the Buddhist community, so I was deemed to be the best choice for writing the diary, to keep a true record of the process of the Ceremony of Ordination.

As a result, I was put in a position to work busily, running around in circles. I had to attend all classes and activities, to take care of the whole place, being mindful of the whole process, and be the first to arrive and the last to leave. I had to get up early in the morning, sleep late at night, with no break time for resting during the day. For every class, I could not be lazy or fall asleep like some other Dharma brothers; otherwise, the precepts masters would scold me and the Dharma brothers would blame me. Just like the saying, "the rafters that stick out get worn down first," I felt like I was being pointed at and seen by everyone, and under the public eyes there was nowhere to hide.

However, these two roles and duties trained my physique, faith, and the ability to deal with people and things. At the same time, it enhanced my need to improve my studies. After forty days of training, at the time the ordination ceremony was completed, I was probably the one who gained the most among the hundred or more applicants for receiving the precepts. Not only did I memorize all the rules of the Ordination Hall and the schedule of activities, I also wrote them down in the diary. And I recorded the lectures given by every precepts master, as well as their explanations for the precepts. For example, I summarized the contents of *The Essence of the Vinaya Manual, Dharmagupta Bhikshunipratimoksha*, and the *Brahma Net Sutra's Bodhisattva Precepts*. In the end, I completed the *Diary of the Ordination Platform* in nearly 130,000 words, and handed it to Haihui Temple for publishing as the enduring reference and memory for the people related to the ordination ceremony. Even today, when I read that diary, I still feel new and refreshed.

Before we walked out of the Ordination Hall and left the mountain, our training master, Venerable Baisheng, knew that during the ordination ceremony, I worked very hard yet was unable to take care of everything, so I still received some criticisms and complaints. He consoled me with these lines in front of the public: "Don't be the head of the shramaneras when receiving ordination. Living and movements are restricted and not free. Once hated by the Dharma brothers and scolded by the precepts master, one can only turn the flowing of tears inwards."

I was very grateful to the Venerable for being compassionate and caring to me. However, I was not very satisfied with what I heard and saw in the Ordination Hall. Because the precepts masters mostly recited what was written in the books, they simply repeated what people in ancient times had said or done; what the students did not understand, the precepts masters probably didn't either. Especially the terms in the teachings of the sila and vinaya were often transliterated from Sanskrit; there were no such things or events in Chinese culture, so they could not be properly explained in Chinese. In addition, the ancient Chinese often used indirect ways to explain the various problems in the teaching of sila and vinaya.

Modern people who lack the academic foundation and cultural background of ancient scholars would not be able to understand [these issues of the precepts]. In the Ordination Hall, the new applicants for receiving the precepts did not ask. They simply listened to the precepts masters, and when they heard parts they didn't understand, or that didn't make sense, they thought it should be that way. I often found it inconvenient to ask questions in class, and would ask the precepts masters after class. Only Master Daoyuan said to the group more than once: "The sila and vinaya are very hard to understand, so it is very difficult to teach the vinaya. I hope all of you will be inspired to study the vinaya texts and spread the teaching." I discovered at the time—whether it be the Buddhist precepts for the monks or for lay people, for shravakas or for bodhisattvas—not only should we make a great effort to clarify their meanings, but also to revise and adapt them for the modern world and current society. Otherwise, it would be like holding onto dead prescriptions to help cure changing diseases. That would be merely emphasizing the vinaya that lacked the actual function of purifying society and human minds. This was the reason why after receiving the ordination, I earnestly worked on memorizing and reciting the *Dharmagupta Bhikshupratimoksha* and *Brahma Net Sutra's Bodhisattva Precepts*. It also became my motivation for studying the vinaya shortly afterwards. I hoped to understand the precepts myself first, and then let others be able to understand them, also. To try them on myself first and then let others try them.

Chapter 4

The Vinaya and the Agamas

The Study of Vinaya Was Not Difficult

In the autumn of 1961, after receiving the three-stage full ordination, I returned to the Chung-Hwa Institute of Buddhist Culture in Beitou where Master Dongchu resided. I stayed there for less than a week and then I resigned as editor of *Humanity* and requested leave from Master Dongchu to prepare for my study of the vinaya in the mountains in southern Taiwan. Although the Master didn't want me to leave, he couldn't stop me either. However, when I prostrated to him and earnestly asked for leave, he seemed very happy. He gave me some brief words of advice and a stack of dollar bills in case I needed money in the mountains.

Where I went—Guanglin Village, Meinong Township in Kaohsiung County—transportation was inconvenient and material conditions were very poor, but the scenery was beautiful. The mountain was called Jian Shan (Sharp Mountain) and the people at the monasteries called it Daxiong Shan (Magnificent Mountain). The name of the monastery was Daxiong Shan Chaoyuan Monastery (the formal name includes the word "monastery"). Residing there were only a seventy-year-old monk, a few nuns, and some lay women. Since transportation was inconvenient, it was not a popular place for pilgrimage, and it wasn't a monastery relying on performing ritual ceremonies for income; instead, it relied on growing lichee trees and bamboo. It was a monastery with a *nong chan* (farming and Chan) atmosphere, so it was very quiet.

However, today, it is one of the tourist highlights in Kaohsiung, known as the Yellow Butterfly Valley. At the time, scarcely more than a few people visited the monastery in a month, so it was my good fortune to stay there. However, during one period I had no money to buy toothpaste, toothbrush, soap, or even stamps for corresponding with the outside world. Luckily, in the mountains it was warm in the winter, cool in the summer and every day was a good day. I still cherish the time I spent there, and it should have been a very important stage in my life, since I went there to cultivate and regulate my body and mind. First, I practiced the *Great Compassion Repentance*, then the *Amitabha Repentance*, then the *Lotus Sutra Repentance*. Besides the morning and evening services, I also had morning and evening sittings, and I spent more time on the sittings.

However, I continued to read and write. Due to the feelings I had in the Ordination Hall, I aspired to read the vinaya texts first. Chaoyuan Monastery also bought a set of the *Taisho Tripitaka* from the Chung-Hwa Institute of Buddhist Culture. Its three volumes— 22, 23, and 24—all belonged to the vinaya section. And my Dharma brothers, whom I knew from the ordination, also mailed me several hard-to-find single-copied vinaya works, and none of them were collected in the vinaya section of the *Taisho Tripitika*. Especially the *Expanded Edition of Thirty Three Kinds of Vinaya Study Works Collected by Master Hongyi*, which my Dharma brother Master Jingkong lent me, and which gave me the chance to indulge blissfully in the vast sea of vinaya texts.

I first wrote two articles which were later collected in *Buddhist Culture and Literature*: "How to Become the Ideal Lay Bodhisattva— After Reading the *Sutra on Upasaka Precepts*," written in June, 1961;

and "Reflections on the *Expanded Edition of Thirty Three Kinds of Vinaya Study Works Collected by Master Hongyi*," written in March, 1962. At that time, I already had this view regarding the bodhisattva precepts: "the *Mangala Sutra* said, bodhisattvas have precepts that could be broken, and the non-Buddhists have no precepts to be broken. Breaking the precepts is still better than not having any precepts to break. After receiving the bodhisattva precepts, one gives rise to the bodhi-mind. Though one who broke the precepts may end up with severe karma and retribution, yet in the future, since one had received the bodhisattva precepts, one would ultimately become a true bodhisattva and attain the highest buddhahood. As a result, I hope that the lay disciples would make the highest aspiration to ask for bodhisattva precepts." (From "Reflections on the *Sutra on Upasaka Precepts*—How to Become the Ideal Lay Bodhisattva" collected in *Buddhist Culture and Literature*.)

I haven't changed that way of thinking even till the present day. What Chinese Buddhism referred to as the Mahayana path was also the bodhisattva path. The Mahayana belief is that the path of practicing Buddhism and becoming a buddha must go through the stages of the bodhisattvas. To give rise to the utmost bodhi-mind, one must begin with the cultivation of the bodhisattva path, and if one does not receive the bodhisattva precepts, that would be very inconsistent.

Regarding the vinaya thoughts of Master Hongyi (1880-1942), I also had this view: "The ancient masters often made descriptions without establishing their own views. This was to show the rigorousness in stating one's opinions, and to show respect towards the sacred teachings. As a result, in Master Hongyi's works, he mostly did the work of organization and arrangement, and complemented them with comments. He would add his own comments and explanations only when absolutely essential, and this did not reach the purpose of teaching and introducing the materials. Although his vinaya thoughts were based on the ancient texts, they avoided the pitfall of holding onto ancient views, which was most difficult and praiseworthy." (From "Reflections on the *Expanded Edition of Thirty Three Kinds of Vinaya Study Works Collected by Master Hongyi*" collected in *Buddhist Culture and Literature.*)

When I read any book, I paid special attention to the utilization of the source materials and the accuracy of its explanations. However, I also paid attention to what the writer was trying to convey, whether the writer could gain new insights through restudying old materials, pointing out the differences and similarities, and set up a reasonable guideline and direction for one to follow. I also hoped to avoid "swallowing ancient teachings without digesting" or "solely talking about things generated by myself."

For any knowledge, practice makes perfect, otherwise it would be hard to become familiar and skillful at the things that are foreign to us. I was not particularly interested in the vinaya, but everyone said that it was hard to understand, so I tried to understand it. When I first read the larger vinaya texts, I read the shastras (commentaries) on the vinayas, then I read the *Vinaya Pitaka*, which included: *Mahishasaka (Five Categories) Vinaya, Dharmagupta (Four Categories) Vinaya, Mahasamghika Vinaya, Sarvastivada (Tenfold) Vinaya, Mulasarvastivada Vinaya*, etc. They were around thirty, forty, fifty, sixty volumes each, their contents were thick and complicated, the terms seemed unfamiliar, and the details were trivial. However, when I studied the vinaya, I would first memorize line-by-line all the preceptive characteristics for the bhikshus and bhikshunis, then read one text after another. I used the *Dharmagupta Vinaya* as the basis, and compared the other vinaya texts with it to find out the differences between them.

Even though I didn't understand Sanskrit at the time, after cross-reading, and thorough research and filtering, I gradually understood what those transliterated vinaya terms conveyed, represented, and what their functions were. They were mainly names of people, places, items, and events. Of course they were also transliterated to reflect their multiple meanings, but unlike Tantric Buddhism that used transliterations because they were secret and not to be spoken. As for what appeared to be complicated rules and guidelines, if you categorized them into a way of living, from individual to community, from within the monastery to outside the monastery, from concepts to actions, and put them all together, they were merely what was happening on hand and around us in the daily life of the sangha.

However, one should have the attitude of not using our current living environment to judge the vinaya texts. One should instead turn the current living environment backwards in time for 2,500 years, back to the sangha in Shakyamuni Buddha's time, and live as they did, then one would find it all normal. For example, a country boy who had not seen the world, who is sent to a very modern school may find it difficult to adjust at first, but would gradually get used to it. Therefore, I say that studying the vinaya was not difficult.

The Vinaya Suitable for Modern Times

From 1961 to 1964 in the mountains in Kaohsiung, I read all the sila and vinaya related works I could gather at the time. The more important texts, I read two or three times, making notes as I read, and organized them into categories. Initially, I wasn't planning to write a systematic vinaya work. I only had the motivation to write. I submitted an article to the *Everlasting Light* magazine in Southeast Asia, and published a work related to the vinaya. Master Zhumo, the person in charge of the magazine, encouraged me and sent ten US dollars to me; he also said that he would print the article and make it into small booklets for distribution. After I wrote the book on vinaya studies, I received further promises from him that he was willing to sponsor me if I had no funds to publish the book. Perhaps it was under such encouragement that I wrote one article after another, and by 1965, I accumulated enough articles to make them into a book. I passed them to the Buddhist Culture Service Center of Master Xingyun for publishing, and that was the *Essentials of Buddhist Sila and Vinaya* (Chn. *Jieluxue gangyao*), which was written in 190,000 words.

The book was divided into seven sections as follows: *Introduction, Taking Refuge in the Three Jewels, The Five Precepts and Ten Virtues, The Eight Precepts, The Ten Shramanera Precepts and The Six Shiksamana Rules, The Essentials of Bhikshu and Bhikshuni Precepts, The Essentials of Bodhisattva Precepts*. What kind of book was it? In its *Author's Preface* I mentioned the following: "I was attempting to revive the silas and vinayas, rather than teach them in the old manner. Of course, my purpose was to seek commonality without making the readers feel bored, and to introduce and answer some of the major questions regarding the vinaya. The book quoted important sources from the vinaya texts as well as the commentaries from ancient masters. It also made an effort to account for the sources to allow the reader to make further studies or research. In fear of the readers not being able to understand certain technical terms quoted from the original texts, bracketed explanations were moderately provided. The characteristic of the book is practical, common, and a work of research."

In the past, anyone studying the vinaya would maintain his or her own sectarian position, and even the contemporary Master Hongyi was not an exception. As for my book, I was only introducing the Buddhist precepts, without considering whether I was the heir of the Nanshan Vinaya Master Daoxuan (596-667) of the *Dharmagupta Vinaya*. I dared not say that I had full understanding of the vinaya, but I would always try my best to maintain a position of not taking a position, to clearly present the spirit of the precepts that were established by Shakyamuni Buddha. To introduce them to the people in modern society, and let them understand and be willing to use the precepts. In the *Author's Preface* I said: "Generally speaking, the book was greatly influenced by Masters Ouyi (1599-1655) and Hongyi, but it did not follow their directions entirely nor completely address them from the standpoint of the Nanshan lineage."

Due to the publishing of *The Essentials of Buddhist Sila and Vinaya*, many people aspired to take refuge in the Three Jewels, become monks, or receive bodhisattva precepts. The book was also used as the text for the classes of several Buddhist Academies. The Jinling Scripture Printing House in Nanjing in Mainland China also reprinted the book for distribution. Another thing worth mentioning was that in the past, people who studied the vinaya would be referred to as Precepts Masters, and they would also see themselves as Precepts Masters. However, although the two masters from the Ming Dynasty—Ouyi and Lianchi (1532-1612)—also wrote works related to vinaya studies, they were not viewed as Precepts Masters. As for myself, although I studied the vinaya, I do not consider myself a Precepts Master, and I was not publicly recognized by others as one. I was only following in accord with the Buddha's rule that a monk should at the minimum know about the living guidelines, and understand the meaning of the "allowable, forbidden, upholding, and violating" of the vinaya, which was the common knowledge that every monk should have.

The *Agamas* Were the Basis of Buddhadharma

When I studied the vinaya, I discovered at the same time that to fully understand the vinaya, one must also thoroughly understand the *Agamas*. The so-called five vinaya sects were formed because, after Shakyamuni Buddha entered nirvana his disciples traveled to different parts of India to spread the Dharma. Due to India's complex languages, dialects, and differences in the ethnic backgrounds, the teachings of the Dharma were categorized to adapt to different regions and environments, and this naturally formed the so-called Sectarian Buddhism. Every sect had its own transmission of sutras and vinaya. At the time, there were eighteen or twenty or more Buddhist sects in India. There should have been that many different sets of vinayas and agamas, however, in the present day, we could only see four vinayas and five shastras remaining, and there were only four *Agamas*.

There were two motives for me to study the *Agamas*: First, the vinaya often used the term *zheng fa lu* (the right Dharma and vinaya) and mentioned that "when the vinaya exists in the world, the Dharma exists in the world," which means that the vinaya and the Dharma cannot be separated. The *Agamas* clearly depicted the Dharma, and the *Vinaya* clearly depicted the precepts. It is clear that the right Dharma is the right vinaya. The right Dharma was said in light of the erroneous Dharma and the right vinayas were said in light of the erroneous vinayas. There is Dharma in the vinaya and vice versa. For example, the vinaya often said: "Be content, lessen desires, and have a sense of shame." This was actually part of the Dharma. And the Dharma said: "the right speech, the right livelihood, and the right action," which were essentially precepts. Therefore, when I was discussing the precepts, I also read the *Agamas*, which included the first and second volumes of the *Taisho Tripitika*. The so-called four *Agamas* included: *Dirgha (Long Sayings) Agama, Madhyama (Middle Length Sayings) Agama, Ekottara (Increased by One Sayings) Agama,* and *Samyukta (Kindred Sayings) Agama*.

Second, reading Master Yinshun's *Introduction to Buddhism*, I noticed his own way of organizing, re-categorizing and systematically introducing the content of the *Agamas*. The Dharma he talked about was all included in the *Agamas*. The later developments in the thoughts of Mahayana Buddhism were also based on the *Agamas*. This was unlike the introduction to Buddhism and Buddhist studies written or compiled by other ordinary scholars, who separated the Mahayana and Hinayana Buddhism, and divided them into sects, schools, and systems.

When I read the *Agamas*, I made many flash cards by collecting similar terms, ideas, and concepts and grouped them into the same category. For example, the same term and concept may appear at different places, and had different expressions and functions. There were the "same group with different meanings" and the "different groups with the same meaning." For example the "dhyana state of the arhats" appeared at different places and had different descriptions. Only by combining them could one have a full scope of understanding and tell what the main points were. Another example would be the meaning of "the sangha as the Three Jewels," the explanations for the Three Jewels itself, as well as the meaning of seeking refuge in the sangha, and exactly what one was taking refuge in. These may all appear at different places, and we could get the final conclusion by combining them. Of course such flash cards were for self-study purposes only. At the time, nobody taught me the methods of how to study and the skills of taking notes. The flash cards may appear to be building indexes and compiling a dictionary, but actually it was not the same. It may be good for me to use them but for others, it may not be a dictionary at all.

I didn't think about writing a book with the knowledge gained from my studies of the *Agamas*, so the pile of notes often stayed with me as I traveled around. It was good to keep them by my side because, when I was thinking about certain Dharma questions, besides looking up the dictionaries and original texts, my notes were also the most convenient source material.

Between 1963 and 1964, the lay Buddhist Mr. Zhu Fei of *Bodhi Tree* magazine in Taichung often invited me to submit articles. It was a magazine for lay people, to introduce the correct and real Dharma to people in society. I posed questions and wrote short essays in the format of Q & A to clarify to the public that Buddhism was not superstition but proper belief. I wrote them for two years, with a total of seventy questions, and I mainly based them on the *Agamas*. In January 1965, I also handed them to the Buddhist Culture Service Center for publishing and distribution as *Orthodox Chinese Buddhism*. I wrote in the *Author's Preface* such explanations: "Nineteen hundred years have passed since Buddhism entered China from India, and the entire culture of China has been uplifted by Buddhist culture. Yet the fundamental spirit of Buddhism was submerged and lost in the native folk customs and bizarre myths of gods and demons. So in recent times, many Chinese with some modern education regard Buddhism as low-class superstition, full of preposterous myths about ghosts and goblins. As a result, this compelled me to pose seventy seemingly simple yet important questions about Buddhism, which were based on my own research, referencing some of the views of Master Taixu and Master Yinshun, and written in accord with the demands of the contemporary age."

Currently, the book is a popular best-seller within the Buddhist community with over 1,000,000 copies in print. Besides being published all over Taiwan, it is also distributed throughout Hong Kong, Southeast Asia, Europe, and the United Sates. One can find this book wherever there are Chinese Buddhists. Even in Mainland China, the book has been published in simplified Chinese characters and distributed continuously since 1980. That was how the Agamas assisted me and enhanced my basic belief in Buddhism.

Chapter 5

Religion and History

The War of Religions

From observing and inspecting the records of eminent monks in the history of Chinese Buddhism, those who emphasized the investigation of the vinaya also emphasized the historical facts, and would at the same time set eyes on the religious problems both within and outside the Buddhist community. For example, Master Daoxuan in the Tang dynasty emphasized both history and the vinaya, and left three enduring works: the *Biographies of the Eminent Monks in the Tang Dynasty*, the *Commentaries on the Dharmagupta Vinaya*, and the *Guang Hongming Compendium*. The works of Vinaya Master Sengyou in the Liang dynasty included the *Biographies of the Eminent Monks in the Liang Dynasty*, and the *Hongming Compendium*. Both the *Hongming Compendium* and the *Guang Hongming Compendium* were collections of materials related to the protection of the Dharma, including the distinctions between Confucianism and Buddhism, the distinctions between Taoism and Buddhism, and the distinctions of the etiquette of China and foreign countries. The two masters were well versed in the sutras and the histories; they also read non-Buddhist texts, and their purposes for doing so were to uphold justice and protect the Dharma.

Of course I dared not compare myself with the ancient masters, but I realized that Buddhism as a whole had been contaminated and misunderstood by both the people within and outside the Buddhist community. The people within the Buddhist community did not know how to teach the Dharma, uphold the Three Jewels, have self-respect, re-examine themselves, make introspections, rectify outdated customs and habits, and revive the glory of the Dharma. Society outside the Buddhist community was not only flooded with antireligious materialistic thoughts, but there were also mixed forces of Christianity, Western culture, and technology, which had devastating effects on Buddhism. For example, the contemporary writer Mr. Jiang Menglin and his famous book the *Western Tide*, had this kind of thinking. Just like the saying "confronting internal troubles and outside aggressions," it's no wonder Buddhism was on its decline and could have even perished.

As a result, I paid close attention to things happening within Buddhism as well as Christianity's actions towards Buddhism. After I wrote "Commentary and Refutation of the Comparison between Christianity and Buddhism," I wrote three more articles successively. In 1959, I wrote "Concerning the Religious Belief of the Thoughts of Hu Shi." The *Ching Feng* magazine, published by the Christian Chinese Religion Research Group of Taofong Shan in Hong Kong, obscured the views between Buddhism and Christianity, so I wrote an article called "Discussions on the Similarities and Differences between Christianity and Buddhism." I wrote another article afterwards, "Further Discussions on the Similarities and Differences between Christianity and Buddhism."

Regarding the religious belief of Hu Shi's thoughts, I once said: "Essentially, Mr. Hu Shi himself is anti-religious and non-religious, and he is also an atheist and nihilist. Although he is not a natural scientist, he believes that other than matter, there is no such thing as a soul. So he attacked the concept of the existence of a soul by saying, 'Religious people often talk about the immortality of the soul. This kind of thinking, over thousands of years, is blindly believed by countless ignorant people, and also believed by many scholars.' He further said, 'The people in the East see the nobles as the ones who have accumulated merits in their previous lives, and the poor would say they are destined to be poor, as they haven't accumulated merits in the past... For most people, their greatest fortune does not come from reciting the Buddha's names but through working hard and struggles.'"

Regarding Mr. Hu Shi's religious thoughts, I made various arguments back and forth to explain that Buddhism was not the way he saw it, or thought about it. I said, "According to history, we could recognize what Mr. Hu Shi referred to as the immortality of history and society, but to further recognize the immortality of a person's individual values (the result of good and bad actions), that would be great independence and great freedom. It is evident that Buddhism is not contrary to Mr. Hu Shi's views, but goes beyond his concepts... Buddhism was originally a religion with wisdom, and a religion of human culture, especially early Buddhism. For one to learn Buddhism, one must first become a righteous man with good morals."

The Taofong Shan of Christianity in Hong Kong was originally the Chingfeng Shan which retreated from Nanjing, and was one of the sub-branches of the Lutheran Church. They once sent their priests to the Buddhist Chan monasteries, such as the Jinshan Monastery in Zhenjiang, and the Tianning Monastery in Yangzhou. They stayed there to study Chan, practice Chan, and meditated just like pious lay Buddhists. They then established their new group based on what they had learned, heard, and seen from the monasteries, and used the Christian concepts and beliefs to explain Buddhism. They further adopted the schedule, rules and way of living in the Buddhist monasteries to conduct Christian style prayers and spiritual practice. Although their ultimate goal was unclear, they had attracted large groups of young monks from the Buddhist sanghas and trained them to become Christian priests. This aroused my sense of crisis about the future of Buddhism. My view was that the Christians could preach, but why did they turn monks into priests? They could certainly teach their vision of the Trinity, the Father, the Son, and the Holy Spirit. But why must they interpret the true suchness, buddha-nature, and Dharma nature of Buddhism as God, the Word, and the Spirit in Christianity? We could tolerate the existence of Christianity; Buddhists often took a friendly attitude in recognizing Jesus as the emanation of a bodhisattva, and that the Christians could deliver the sentient beings who needed their way of teaching. However, it is not necessary to say that Christianity is Buddhism, and that Buddhism is not needed since there is Christianity. We can recognize the fact that Christianity exists, but we cannot tolerate the fact that Buddhism was being devastated. Therefore, I decided to take up the pen and fight, but I was not the one who started this war of religion.

Writing about Christianity

When I was in the mountains in southern Taiwan, I thought I could live in peace without quarrels, and "bury myself" in the Buddhist *Tripitika* and contemporary Buddhist works for several years, to not read the mass newspapers and magazines, no radio, and of course no television. At the time, there were no telephones in the mountains, not even electric lamps. It was a life isolated from society and living in "Utopia."

Unfortunately, the good times never last. Unexpectedly, some kind person brought the Catholic *Hengyi* magazine to where I was staying, and there was an article in it that discussed Buddhism. At the same time, someone gave me several books related to Buddhism written by a priest that graduated from the Correspondence Department of Bukkyo University, as well as some books that refuted Buddhism written by a Catholic Father, who was the professor at Fu Jen Catholic University. Of course, since the books were written by a priest and a Father, they wouldn't have the correct understanding and fair introduction of Buddhism. Actually, their goals and intentions were quite evident. They were directed towards Buddhists, and tried to break their faith by quoting from the sutras and refuting it with the viewpoints stated in the sutras. At the time, there really were not many people from the Buddhist community who read that many sutras and shastras that were able to write articles of such class. People saw that I could write a few articles, so not only did the Buddhists hope to see me refute them, even the Father and priest were challenging publicly by saying, "So the Buddhists should also write something! Who would it be?" They were eager to find a match from the Buddhist community. At the time, Master Zhuyun made several public lectures at the Tainan Park on the topic of comparison between Christianity and Buddhism, and he also published a small booklet. Unfortunately, he was later diagnosed with high blood pressure and diabetes, and experienced recurring headaches and insomnia, and was unable to take up the challenge anymore.

Another elder, Master Yinshun, was originally a Christian, and after he had learned Buddhism for over thirty years, some Christians dared to come to his monastery to challenge him and tried to preach to him. As a result, he wrote two long articles, "God Loves the World" and "Further Discussions on God Loves the World." Since the priest Du Erwei categorized Buddhist belief as a kind of Moon God belief, he wrote another long article titled "The Founding of the Eastern Pure Land."

I was staying in the mountains and didn't want to be bothered, but when the Christians began calling for a challenge publicly, I wanted to clarify their viewpoints, to explain the Buddhist views towards Christianity, and to make clear to ordinary intellects how to face the problems of religion. Of course I did not want to imitate the sectarian attitudes of the Christians and attack Christianity, because Confucius said: "Do not do to others what you don't want to be done to you." However, I wished to use the objective materials to do a fair introduction, so between 1964 and 1966, I wrote articles successively, combined them into a book, and handed it to several Buddhist magazines for publishing. They were *Sound of Sea Tide, Awakening the World,* and *Hong Kong Buddhism.* In 1967, it was handed over to the Buddhist Culture Service Office, and the book was titled *Research on Christianity* (Chn. *Jidujiao zhi yanjiu*), and I wrote in the Author's Preface about my motives, attitudes, and purposes for writing the book:

"The Christians' attacks on Buddhism and call for challenges compelled my interest to do research on Christianity, and I wrote this book as a result. I thank the Christians who attacked Buddhism for the making of this book. In order to write this book, I carefully read over 50 different Chinese and English works. My attitude was to stand in the Western scholars' viewpoint to introduce Western faith and religion. I used the orthodox Christian materials to explain the content of Christianity and its true face, and at the same time I provided objective and reasonable clarifications on certain important questions between Buddhism and Christianity. I had no intention to promote Christianity or attack Christianity. I was just using the historical point of view to inspect, analyze, and research Christianity."

This book was published by the Jiuda Culture Publishing Company in 1987, and listed by the publisher as the seventh book in their Ultimate Care Series. They printed on the cover in small letters the words I said in the book: "God in the minds of Westerners is like a hammock evenly hanging between the shades of two large trees. On one end is the tree of philosophy and on the other end is the bark of science. God is between philosophy and science, but God is neither philosophy nor science yet encompasses the essence of philosophy and science. People lie in the arms of God and find spiritual comfort. Such views of God, most Asian people do not understand and naturally could not comprehend."

As a result, the chief editor of Jiuda wrote at the bottom of the book cover a few lines of his short comment to make the finishing point: "When Christianity walked out of Palestine, over thousands of years they constructed God's unbreakable fortress, and the arena of Christian faith was strongly fortified. Master Sheng Yen faced the challenge of Christians attacking Buddhism, and through his writing, used the tone of reason to untie the knot of different religious views, and paved the way for a more tolerant religious view."

When I published the book, there were two extreme reactions: First, the Buddhist community felt relieved that in the end someone among them understood Christianity and they didn't need to fear the Christians walking into the monasteries distributing the Bible or pamphlets. A certain monk printed Chapter 4 of my book, *How Great is Christianity?* and distributed it as a booklet to various monasteries to give to Christians who came to the monasteries to preach. Secondly, the Father and the priest stopped the pen fight, but it provoked the other Christians, and they viewed me as a pain in the neck. Some of them took my book and criticized it line-by-line, not that they wanted me to respond, but that I should read more. They thought I didn't understand the Bible and didn't get its essence, so they wanted me to repent to God. Some Christians turned to the regular newspapers and magazines, and submitted articles to criticize and ridicule Buddhism.

Three years ago, someone from the Presbyterian Church came to seek refuge in the Three Jewels, and when he met me, he said he had read my book, *Research on Christianity*. I asked him whether he changed his belief because of that and he said: "No, if a Christian read that book, instead of giving praise to it, they would be repelled by it. The essence of Christianity is emphasizing salvation through faith in God, and any philosophical thought or reason would be useless to them. If they do not engage in introspection, they would not alter their belief." So I told him, "I understand. You can say that, rather than targeting the Christians, I wrote that book for the sake of Buddhists and those who don't have religious belief yet."

Comparative Religion

Since the beginning of human culture, there has been the need for religion, and there are religious activities and facts. It is the final resting place for humanity, and the earliest motive force. The belief of each individual's protector god gradually developed into the religion of a monotheistic belief. Therefore, the development of monotheism is the result of the merging of the multiple gods of polytheism. As a result, monotheism is not necessarily the one and only, but the generic term for countless gods. It is not rejecting the countless gods, so there is the one god to solely rule over the truth of the universe.

Due to the dynamics of polytheism, it may appear to be

complicated and superstitious. In addition, due to the arbitrary belief of monotheism and its excluding and conquering characteristics, the intolerance between different religions resulted. These are not the positive values of religion. Unfortunately, since the beginning of human history, people would fight for the material living conditions, and they also would fight for the faith of spiritual life. The God of every religion would tell their followers that there is only one true and righteous God, and that is the one they believe in. In addition, the belief in the other gods or spirits is all evil and demonic. Therefore, they would view the followers of religions other than their own belief as the limbs, incarnation or equivalent of the Demon.

This is due to affirming one's own belief and rejecting what others believe in—only wanting to know what one believes and does and refusing to know the beliefs and actions of other religions. As a result, the religious faith that was originally supposed to bring happiness for humanity resulted in catastrophes due to the enmity between different religions. Such facts could be clearly seen in the New and Old Testaments of Christianity. Between new and traditional religions, the local and foreign religions, as well as the religions between different nations and ethnic groups they were constantly at war with one another. The conflicts occurred not only verbally and theoretically, but also actively, resulting in massive slaughter and blood shed. Even in the 20th century, today there are still some religious and political maniacs who would cry out for the "Holy War."

If different religions could have mutual respect and understanding, lessening the suspicion and hate, and learn from each other, then humanity in the world could really benefit from religious faith and find peace and happiness. Buddhists always have this kind of open mind. In the time of Shakyamuni Buddha, he had told his disciples to respect and support the Buddhist bhikshus and bhikshunis as well as the shramanas and Brahmins of the original and new religions in India. Although there were differences in thoughts, concepts, and practices among religions, the purpose of letting disciples know about these differences is to protect their faith rather than to attack other religions. Even to those who had changed their faith to Buddhism, the Buddha told them to continue their support for the needs of the religious teachers of their prior belief. To support the sangha is a virtue, and to support the practitioners of all religions is also a virtue.

When Buddhism entered China, it was attacked and rejected by the Confucian and Taoist scholars. However, Buddhists tolerated Confucianism and Taoism, and even came up with the theory of the "Same Origin of Three Religions." This resulted in the incorporation of ideas from Confucianism and Taoism into Buddhism. As a result, in the Song and Ming dynasties, the Confucians also incorporated Buddhism into Confucianism. Buddhism did not reject Confucianism and Taoism, but treated them as the humanitarian basis that accommodated with Buddhism. Buddhism first accepted the Chinese culture, then it was accepted by the Chinese culture, and it developed into part of mainstream Chinese culture—Confucianism, Taoism, and Buddhism.

Based on such understandings, besides doing research and writings on Christianity, I also collected materials related to the religions in the world, and advocated for followers of all religions to have the knowledge of comparative religion. I also hoped to compile a kind of introductory reference book for people to use. In the autumn of 1966, I had not yet begun to compile and write the book, but the President of Shoushan Buddhist Institute in Kaohsiung, Master Xingyun, already opened up a class for me to teach comparative religion at the

Buddhist Institute.

So I collected what I could find at the time on all the books and works related to religion that were published in Chinese, Japanese, and translated into Chinese from foreign languages. I wrote as I studied, and after half a year, I completed the book titled *The Study of Comparative Religion* (Chn. *Bijiao zongjiao xue*), and passed it to the Chung Hwa Book Company in Taipei for publishing in 1968. The book, comprising 200,000 words, was divided into ten chapters: Primitive Religion, Religion of the Aboriginals, Religion of the Ancient Tribes, Religion in India, Religion in China, Religion of the Minorities, Judaism, Christianity, Islam, and Buddhism.

I was not satisfied with it for two reasons. First, I didn't do much comparative research, only some explanations on the historical and background relationships, and their origins and development. Secondly, I understood too few foreign languages, so I could not utilize more materials written in foreign languages. Up to the present, it was not known whether someone else had written a better book on comparative religion, and I was not sure how many other religions were left out of my book. After that, I always wanted to write another book [on comparative religion]. However, in a flash of an eye, 24 years have passed by and I no longer have the time to work on this issue. Up until the present day, there is no better book on introductory comparative religion in the domestic market. Since I have too many things to do, and I am getting old, there is no way for me to write another book.

History of World Buddhism

I mentioned before that someone who paid attention to the vinaya would naturally pay attention to history. Actually, to do research on the vinaya, one cannot deviate from history. The vinaya itself is related to the activities of the sangha, and the on-going sangha activities make Buddhist history. If one begins with Buddhist history, it is easy to pay attention to the vinaya because Buddhist history is composed of the events of remarkable monks from the different eras. Being strict in keeping the precepts, following rules orderly (with discipline), and with proper management, outstanding talents among monks could be nourished. They would also earn respect from everyone, who would then come gather around and learn from them. As a result, eminent monks who emphasized the study of history would also attend to the vinaya.

I am neither a Precepts Master nor a historian, but after I discovered the reasons for the decline in contemporary Buddhism, I wanted to learn new things from reviewing old materials, and from tracing the history to gain an insight to develop a bright future for Buddhism. At the same time, I also realized that while Buddhism originated in India, after its circulation for 2,500 years, the schools and sects that have been developed are wide and diverse. It is like a fountain with water running through different locations, the water is mixed with dirt and sand along the way. When the water passes through the Yellow Earth Plateau, it turns brownish yellow; when it passes through black earth, it turns black; when it passes through white earth, it turns white. Which one of these is its original nature? Which one of these are the distinctive additions from different times and places?

Today, we see that there is Theravada Buddhism and Northern Buddhism, and among Northern Buddhism, there is the division of Chinese Buddhism and Tibetan Buddhism. Chinese Buddhism is then divided into areas of China, Japan, Korea, and Vietnam, etc.

And in China, it is further divided into the Ten Sects or Eight Sects. Just within the Chan Sect in China, there are the five lineages and seven schools, so this is very complicated. Today, there should be a common global view to develop a cooperative and compatible modern Buddhism. Otherwise, the Theravada and Northern Buddhism would be competing with each other, and the Chinese and Tibetan Buddhism would be at odds with one another. From the point of view of Buddhism in Japan, Buddhism in China is too conventional. From the point of view of Buddhism in China, Buddhism in Japan is too worldly. In such cases, not only are we failing to spread Buddhism, we are offsetting the efforts made by one another, and that is a pity.

Therefore, I aspired to write a book on the history of world Buddhism, and I completed compiling and writing a book of around one million words titled *History of World Buddhism* (Chn. *Shijie fojiao tongshi*). In my plans, it was to be divided into the first, second, and third volumes. The first volume would include India, Tibet, and Japan, and the second volume would encompass countries in Southeast Asia, Europe, and the American continent. The third volume would cover the Western Regions, China, and Korea. I was hoping to write the text by using the history of the spreading of the sangha as the latitude and the history of the sectarian thoughts as the longitude, to allow the readers to have a clear understanding upon reading this book. To know exactly what new things and thoughts happened at what time, and in what era was there a re-examination and new development of the basic essence of Buddhism. We could grasp the origin and development of Buddhism under changing conditions, and realize the unchangeable basic principles and standards that should be followed by every sect or school in all areas and eras; otherwise, it would not be Buddhism but the "non-Buddhists".

Not only was there no one in China that wrote a similar book as such on the history of world Buddhism, even in the other modern countries in the world, including Japan, nobody had written a book as such. Although between 1960-1970, the Rissho Kosei-kai Publishing Office published a series, *Buddhist History in the Asian Continent* in twenty volumes. The series only included India, China, and Japan, lacking in Tibet, Korea, Europe and the America Continent. From 1966 onwards, I began writing and compiling Indian Buddhist History, followed by Tibetan Buddhist History, and then Japanese, Korean, and Vietnamese Buddhist History. However, in the spring of 1969, I traveled east to Japan, and began my life as a student studying abroad. It was another battlefield that I needed to be prepared for, so I had to put down all my original plans, and put all my efforts in completing the necessary courses for my master's and doctoral degrees, as well as the mandatory thesis.

At the time, I was planning to finish the *History of World Buddhism* after I completed the highest degree. As a result, in August 1969, when I handed the original manuscripts for this book to the Chung Hwa Book Company in Taipei for publishing, it was named the First Volume of the *History of World Buddhism*. Even up to the present day, many people asked me where the second and third volumes are. Was it like the *History of Chinese Philosophy* written by Mr. Hu Shi, that after he wrote the first volume, there were no more to follow?

Every time I thought about this, I would feel very ashamed for not being able to put into action what I have said. Actually, it's not that I didn't want to write, I was forced by conditions to stop writing. Luckily, I already completed nearly 400,000 words, and I also translated a book co-written by five Japanese scholars including

Nogami Shunjo, the *Introduction to the History of Chinese Buddhism.* I handed it to the Commercial Press in Taipei in 1971 for publishing, and it was included in the special No.209 of "Literature for Everyone," with Mr. Wang Yunwu as the chief editor. At least it was better than nothing, and provided much convenience for the readers and myself. Especially the first volume of my *History of World Buddhism* was currently used as the textbook in various Buddhist Academies in Mainland China. I really hoped that one day I would be able to set my mind on realizing my unfulfilled wish!

Chapter 6

Life Studying Abroad

In the Trend of Studying Abroad

In my youth I hadn't thought about the issue of studying abroad because the monks who studied abroad in Japan rarely made any contribution to Chinese Buddhism, and at most they only translated a few books. Compared to the eminent domestic monks who had not studied abroad, such as the four great masters in contemporary Chinese Buddhism—Xuyun, Hongyi, Yinguang (1861-1940), and Taixu—who were revered by the masses, studying abroad appeared to be of not much usefulness. As a result when I came to Taiwan and became a monk again [after leaving the Army], I had not thought about studying in Japan. Although a few young monks of my age with a similar aspiration did go to Japan, and some people encouraged me to follow suit, at the time I did not have the financial support or the wish to do so. Rather, I went to the mountains instead of traveling across the sea.

As a Buddhist monk, to be able to study abroad one should thank the Cardinal Bishop Paul Yu (Yu Bin). He was the chairman of the National Assembly and the President of Fu Jen University, as well as the Bishop of the Roman Catholic Church in the Nanjing District, who later rose to be a cardinal. As a result he had a very influential voice in the Chinese National Government, and it could be said that "his words carry heavy weight." The students of the Faculty of Theology of Fu Jen University were not under the governance of the

Ministry of Education. However, they needed to study abroad, so the Cardinal spoke to the Ministry of Internal Affairs to legalize the plan for religious personnel studying abroad. After it was revealed in the newspaper that groups of their Catholic students went to study abroad, the Buddhist community also followed up and requested the government for equal rights and religious status. Therefore, several young monks were also approved to study abroad in Japan.

In 1975, after I completed my studies in Japan, I returned to Taiwan and attended the Conference of Academic Scholars Studying Abroad. At the conference, I met Cardinal Bishop Paul Yu and I thanked him in person, saying that because of him I was able to study abroad in Japan and completed my degrees. Perhaps he didn't understand why I thanked him, and I wasn't sure if he had thought about letting Buddhists study abroad when he was striving for the legislation. Nevertheless, it was a fact that young Buddhist monks did benefit as a result. From this standpoint, I approved that Buddhists, including monks, should participate in politics and enter the parliaments of various levels of the government to strive for the benefits of Buddhism as well as providing wisdom to the entire society.

After I entered the mountains for a few years, a lay Buddhist Mr. Yang Baiyi, who was educated in Bukkyo University in Japan, collected piles of secondhand Buddhist texts from the used book stands on Guling Street in Taipei, and sent them to my "solitary confinement" from time to time. The so-called solitary confinement was the small living quarters I was staying in, which was concealed, and its only connection with the outside world was a small window that allowed people to send food and daily supplies. Within the six years I stayed in the mountains, I went into solitary retreat twice.

During that period, I also started studying Japanese grammar books, and was able to read Japanese through self-study, which enabled me to deal with source materials in Japanese. [During this time] I wrote a few books. As far as I was concerned at the time, I thought it would be enough to understand Japanese and utilize the works written in Japanese, and there was no need for me to go to Japan.

Afterwards, because at the time the Christian magazines were openly challenging the Buddhist community by saying that none of the Chinese Buddhists could really understand Sanskrit, one of the original languages of Buddhism. They claimed that if the Buddhists only understood Chinese and not Sanskrit that would be like worlds away because they could only guess instead of truly understanding the meaning of Buddhadharma. Unlike the Catholic fathers or clergy, who took a mandatory course of studying the Holy Bible every day in Latin. After being provoked by this, even though I was nearly forty years old, I still had the courage to say, "Who else would do it but I?" At the same time, Mr. Zhang Mantao, a good friend of mine who was currently studying in Kyoto Japan, often wrote me long letters discussing religion, philosophy, Buddhist studies and Buddhadharma, as well as global events and historical events. In his letters, he would always encourage me to go to Japan no matter what, and that even to go there to breathe the fresh air would be nice.

Furthermore, my Tonsure Master Dongchu also approved my studying abroad, which I really did not expect. The domestic Buddhist education was generally poor; the monks were seen as unimportant by ordinary people, and they did not have degrees in higher education. They were even forbidden to go to various colleges and universities to teach the Buddhist youths. In order to improve the quality of monks and the academic status of Buddhism, and be in preparation for establishing a new phase of Buddhist education, I was determined to study abroad in Japan. Actually, after reading many Japanese Buddhists works, I discovered that there was glorious success in terms of the Buddhist education facilities and academic research in Japan, and it had become one of the leaders in the movements of world Buddhism.

So in February 1968, I walked out of my solitary retreat and the mountains of Meinong town in Kaohsiung and arrived in Taipei. I temporarily stayed at the foremost monastery at the time, Shandao Temple. I used one year's time to prepare for reading and writing the Japanese language; at the same time I also hosted the Buddhist Culture Lectures every Sunday. I was in charge of teaching the sutras and shastras, and would also give lectures on specific topics occasionally. The more popular among the sutras and shastras were the *Awakening of Mahayana Faith* and the *Verses Delineating the Eight Consciousnesses*. Among the lectures on specific topics, the ones that were organized into manuscripts were *The Value of Chinese Buddhist Arts*, and *The Epics of Guanyin Bodhisattva*. During this period, I published *The Study of Comparative Religion*, and I also traveled to various places to give lectures, including the School of Theology established by the Presbyterian Church in Yangming Mountain. I no longer used sharp tones and harsh words to speak on Christianity. I also spent some time studying the works of the systems of Chinese Buddhism, including the commentaries on the *Shurangama Sutra*, *The Sutra of Complete Enlightenment, the *Diamond Sutra, and* the Awakening of Mahayana Faith*, as well as the Records of Sayings from the Chan Sect.

First Arrival in Tokyo

At the time, none of the Buddhist youths from Taiwan who studied in Japan had completed their studies and returned, so after some consideration my master also opposed my studying abroad. Also, the overseas Buddhist from Southeast Asia who promised me financial support changed his mind. At the time the Shandao Temple had no obligation to support me. When I left from Taipei to Tokyo on March 14, 1969, other than an air ticket, I was virtually penniless. I marched out on the quest to study abroad amidst the sea of opposing voices from the domestic Buddhist community. Some people were waiting to see me make a fool of myself and some people were truly worried for me. However, I didn't have the sentiment of "Jing Ke assassinates the King of Qin" (Jing Ke was determined to sacrifice himself in his attempt to assassinate the tyrannical King of Qin for the benefit of the people). Nor did I see myself as "the hero who left, never to return." I only thought: if Chinese Buddhism was supposed to decline, and if I did not have the merit to receive any financial support after going abroad, then I could come back anytime and stay in the mountains again, which would also be nice.

When I first arrived in Tokyo, I went to Rissho University in Shinagawa district to complete the admission procedures at the Faculty of Buddhist Studies and be prepared for class. When I entered the classroom, I discovered that I was the oldest. The Japanese classmates were only twenty or so years old, and I was already thirty-nine. I thought about Master Yijing (635–713) in the Tang Dynasty, who went to study abroad in India. He was also thirty-nine years old at the time, so I felt a little more consoled. Two years passed by and I didn't really understand what was being said in the classes. The professors were really nice and friendly, and the Japanese classmates were also very friendly. Some of them lent me their notes for me to copy, and some of them would give me a photocopy of their notes after class. Through my friend's introduction, I had three Japanese tutors to teach me Japanese, and all three of them did so for free. Among them, the most memorable was Prof. Ushiba Shingen, who specialized in teaching Chinese grammar. He was already seventy years old and retired at home. He often thought about ways to repay Chinese Buddhism because he knew that Japan had received great beneficence from Buddhist culture, and that the origin of Japanese Buddhism was in China. The large quantities of the original Chinese texts of Japanese Buddhism also came from China. During World War II, the Japanese attacked the Chinese people, and invaded China. Therefore, he took care of us Chinese monks with shame and gratitude. Every time I went to his house for tutoring, he would treat us with tea and desserts and even served us lunch and dinner.

Another moving story that was facilitated by Prof. Ushiba happened during my study in Japan. It happened in 1973, when he translated Master Yinshun's *History of Chinese Chan* into Japanese, and acted on the Master's behalf to apply for the doctoral degree of Rissho University. I did all the miscellaneous tasks, and Prof. Ushiba was responsible for all the contacting affairs. Although he didn't know Master Yinshun, to show gratitude towards Chinese Buddhism he did everything voluntarily. In that year he made possible the first scholar monk with a doctorate in China. Although this may not be something of significance to Master Yinshun, it was important in terms of raising the status of Buddhism both domestically and internationally. I also felt that it was very important, so I wrote a special article for this event, "Epoch-making Scholar Monk with Doctoral Degree" for publishing in Taiwan.

After half a year more, I could somewhat understand spoken Japanese and I could make notes, and participate in taking turns in the speaking practices in class. After the second semester of the first year, I already completed three quarters of all the required course credits. In the first semester of the second year, I only needed to take one quarter of the course credits, and with the remaining time, I could focus on writing my master's thesis.

Although my foreign language skills were poor both in Japanese and English, I also took Sanskrit and Tibetan courses. However, the teachers taught Sanskrit in Japanese, so how could I learn Sanskrit if I didn't understand Japanese? After a year I could understand elementary Sanskrit grammar, and since I was studying it, I also translated a basic Sanskrit grammar textbook into Chinese for the purpose of teaching it in Taiwan. Unfortunately, after mailing it to a certain Buddhist magazine in Taiwan for publishing for several issues, the chief-editor was replaced, and due to the trouble of proofreading Sanskrit, they stopped publishing it. After continuous search, the original manuscripts were not to be found. My Sanskrit was still poor, and my Japanese writing skill was also poor. As a result, my advisor Prof. Sakamoto Yukio of the Huayan Studies department suggested that as an older Chinese student who started late, it was not impossible for me to specialize in Indian Buddhism but that would take much more time, so it would be better to write on a topic on Chinese Buddhism.

Master's Thesis

Prof. Sakamoto was teaching the famous work *The Mahayana Shamatha-Vipashyana Practice* written by the First Patriarch of the Chinese Tiantai sect, Chan Master Huisi (515-577). When Prof.

Sakamoto gave lectures he often encountered "the tiger blocking the way" (difficulties), of course he could explain them the Japanese way, but since I was Chinese, he often confirmed with me whether he was right or simply asked me for the correct way to say them. In China, regarding the exegesis for this book, I knew there were three of them: 1) Master Liaoran's *Zongyuan Ji of The Mahayana Shamatha-Vipashyana Practice* in the Song Dynasty, 2) Master Ouyi's *Explanations on the Mahayana Shamatha-Vipashyana Practice* in the Ming Dynasty, and 3) The contemporary Master Dixian's *Account of the Mahayana Shamatha-Vipashyana Practice*. I also had a copy of the latter book on hand. When he asked, I would answer. Although what I answered wasn't my own views, he was still quite satisfied.

I asked him about the topic of my master's thesis but he didn't have any opinions. I asked him whether it would be fine to use the topic of *A Study of the Mahayana Shamatha-Vipashyana Practice*. He said fine. Therefore, within half a year, in the first semester of 1971, I studied the original text of *The Mahayana Shamatha-Vipashyana Practice*, as well as its commentaries. I often went to the libraries of Buddhist related universities in Tokyo and Kyoto, such as the University of Tokyo, Toyo University, Taisho University, Komazawa University and Rissho University to search, read, copy, and photocopy related resources. In order to search for the old Japanese magazines before War World II in the Meiji Era (1868-1912), I went to the Naritasan Library in the outskirts of Tokyo. Honestly speaking, too few Japanese scholars did research on *The Mahayana Shamatha-Vipashyana Practice*. Although there were only a few short theses, when I began writing my thesis there were still many resources and materials for me to utilize. My master's thesis had three chapters: "The Organization and Content of *The Mahayana Shamatha-Vipashyana*

Practice"; "The Truthfulness of *The Mahayana Shamatha-Vipashyana Practice* and its Author"; and "The Basic Thoughts of *The Mahayana Shamatha-Vipashyana Practice.*"

In China, there was no doubt that *The Mahayana Shamatha-Vipashyana Practice* was written by Chan Master Nanyue Huisi. However, between the 12th and 13th century, the Japanese Tiantai scholar Master Shoshin listed many reasons stating that it did not appear to be Master Huisi's work. Afterwards, many people also discussed this issue, but Master Shoshin's points were still the most representative. In China, nobody raised similar doubts, and I couldn't agree with Master Shoshin's views, so I proposed a rebuttal.

The greatest benefit I received from writing this thesis was not proving that *The Mahayana Shamatha-Vipashyana Practice* was indeed written by Master Huisi, but learning how to search, utilize, distinguish, and choose the resource materials, and then use them to write a thesis. At the same time, in Chapter 3, I researched and analyzed the origin and source of the thought basis of *The Mahayana Shamatha-Vipashyana Practice*, and I was able to delve more deeply into six sutras and shastras that were most related to this book: *Tathagatagarbha Sutra, Shrimala Devi Sutra, Lankavatara Sutra, Buddhagotra Shastra, Commentary to the Mahayana Samuparigraha Shastra*, and The *Awakening of Mahayana Faith*. This allowed me to gain some understanding of the thoughts of the Tathagatagarbha system and the Yogachara (Consciousness-Only) system. Before I went to Japan, I already knew from the works of Master Taixu and Master Yinshun that there were three systems in Indian [Mahayana] Buddhism: Madhyamaka, Yogachara, and Tathagatagarbha. However, although I read them, but without going through my own experience of analyzing and writing about them, it would be like only skimming over the surface.

When I completed my master's thesis and handed it to my advising professor, he said only one sentence: "Great contents but the wordings were not quite Japanese style." As a result, I invited Prof. Sato Tatsugen of the Komazawa University and Prof. Ushiba Shingen to help me with the smoothing of the language. Prof. Sakamoto was quite pleased with the final version. He encouraged me by saying that it was not easy that I could complete a thesis with 100,000 words within the short half a year. Master Dongchu wanted me to send a written copy of the thesis back to Taiwan for publishing by the *Sound of Sea Tide* magazine. Perhaps he thought that I wrote it in Chinese, so to show him that I was not sleeping in Tokyo and really studying, in the second semester of the second year, I translated it into Chinese, and mailed the chapters serially to Taiwan. The translation for the whole book was completed in October 1971, and published by Dong Chu Publishing House in 1979.

Chapter 7

Views from Every Aspect of Japanese Buddhism

Buddhist Religious Activities

After I completed my master's degree in Japan, there were not many mandatory course credits for the doctoral degree program. The requirement was that the courses be completed between the second and third year, and one could make up for the course credits even in the fourth year. As a result, the time required for attending lectures was a lot less, and many students studying abroad could take a full time job outside of school while they studied for the doctorate courses. Some people even took up several jobs, especially given that the summer vacations were very long, unlike in the United States where they had three or even four semesters in a year. The Taiwanese students studying in Japan would mostly use the long summer vacation to return home to visit relatives, deal with personal affairs, or go on vacation and travel in groups. I wanted to save money on the vacation costs, and instead used the time outside of studies to better understand Japan and the Buddhist religious activities in Japan.

After the Meiji Era, Japanese Buddhism over the recent hundred years became completely worldly, but they still kept the systems well and were able to continue to develop steadily. Japan was a very utilitarian country, so there must be reasons why Buddhism had room to survive and still be respected in that kind of environment. If Japanese Buddhism really were like what the Chinese Buddhists sneered at—having only the core concepts of Buddhism and no real practice—then it wouldn't have been accepted and survived until today. The Chinese would view other Buddhist systems as not ideal. For example: First, Tibetan Buddhism was being called the Buddhism of the buddhas because "living buddhas" could be seen everywhere, and anyone could become a buddha in the present life. Second, Japanese Buddhism was the Buddhism of the Dharma because many scholars were doing research on the Dharma, but nobody really practiced, and they didn't believe in the Buddha or the sangha. Third, Buddhism in Sri Lanka, Burma, and Thailand was the Buddhism of the sangha. In the Buddhism of the Theravada system, sangha members could be seen everywhere. They did not believe that people could become a buddha, and the Buddhist followers only knew about sustaining the sangha, not learning the Dharma. So these were all not ideal. Only Chinese Buddhism had the Buddha, the Dharma, and the Sangha—all of the Three Jewels—intact.

Actually, from my point of view, the Buddhism of all three systems had many talents. Not only within their countries where they established high-level Buddhist education, but they also sent talented people to teach the Dharma abroad. For example, there were twenty or more Buddhist-related universities and institutes in Japan; there were Buddhist universities in Sri Lanka, and there were also two universities founded by the sangha in Thailand. The three major monasteries in Lhasa in Tibet essentially had university organization and content, and monks of the Geluk school must have twelve years of formal education. Therefore, Buddhists propagated the contemporary international Buddhist activities in these three systems. By comparison, in Chinese Buddhism, the monks were lacking in education standards, their education was not systematic, they received no international language training, and very few of them had expertise in and conducted specialized research. As a result, in terms of practice methods and academic research, Chinese Buddhism fell short of other countries. Not understanding others while saying they are not as good is called "arrogant with a narrow view." Chinese Buddhists may have thought they possessed all Three Jewels, but actually they were very vain and surrounded by crisis.

As a result, when I went to Japan I didn't dare criticize them, and only wished to observe and learn from them with an attitude of showing neither inferiority nor superiority. I was hoping to have wide contact with all aspects of Japanese Buddhism, to learn from their strengths and make up for our own shortcomings, and I wouldn't show off myself and demean others. Therefore, I would make full use of the vacation time to visit and participate in all kinds of Buddhist activities.

When my language skills were good enough to converse with Japanese people, I discovered that in their society anyone with secondary education could converse about Buddhadharma for several hours and not seem like amateurs. The reason being that in their elementary and secondary school textbooks, much knowledge related to Buddhism was introduced. At the same time in their newspapers and magazines, you could often find articles by Buddhist scholars or that reported Buddhist-related activities. Whether in the fields of literature, philosophy, arts, religion, and history, all these were affected by Buddhism and Buddhist culture. Therefore, whether they believed in Buddhism or not, ordinary Japanese would not be so unfamiliar with or widely misunderstand Buddhism as most Chinese would.

When in Japan I took part in the traditional as well as the newer Buddhist activities. For the traditional, I went to the Eiheiji Temple in Fukui Prefecture, which was the head temple of the Japanese Soto sect. I also went to their Sojiji Temple in the Tsurumi District of Tokyo, as well as the Engakuji Temple and Kenchoji Temple of the Kamakura Rinzai sect, the Toshoji Temple of the Ryutakuji school in Tokyo, and the Myoshinji Temple of the Rinzai sect in Kyoto. I also stayed overnight for several days in Koyasan of the Shingon sect, and visited the Enryakuji Temple in Hieizan of the Tendai sect. I also had very close contacts with Tendai monks who practiced the 12-year program in the mountains (called *juni-nen-rozangyo*) at the Enryakuji Temple. The Nichiren sect in today's Japan could be counted as traditional Buddhism. Since I was studying at Rissho University, which was founded by their sect, of course most of my friends were monks from that sect. As a result, I also went several times for meetings and practice to the mountain of their head monastery, Minobusan in Yamanashi Prefecture. I visited and took part in the activities of some newly formed Buddhist communities such as the Soka Gakkai Society, which belonged to the Taiseki Temple in Fuji Mountain of the Nichiren Shoshu sect, and the Rissho Koseikai Society in Tokyo, the Kodoshan Society in Yokohama in the outskirts of Tokyo, and also the Kokuchukai Society, Reiyukai Society, Tenrikyo Society, Konkoukyo Society, and Taien Mikkyo Society. At various times, I spent at least a day, several days, or several weeks participating in their practices and observing their activities. They didn't keep any secrets and were very friendly to Chinese monks from Taiwan, offering free meals and living accommodations; they also sent a person to transport me by car.

Of course most of them hoped that I could accept and take back their teachings to Taiwan. However, it was not that easy. It would require spending lots of time to understand, learn, participate, and to put forth full effort. However, through making such quick tours, I could only learn some of their strengths, concepts, and read some of their historical process and methods of operation. The only difference was that I saw them with my own eyes, and being there in person was not quite the same as just reading books.

Historically, Japanese Buddhism was really quite traditional and conservative. In their mountains and monasteries, they kept the rules passed on from the patriarchs. Although the rules were not that strictly followed today, they were not abandoned, and they would at least appear to keep them. For example, in the front door of many old monasteries, there were stone tablets set up by the patriarchs with the inscription "No meat and alcohol." Although it had already become an open fact that they indeed drank alcohol and ate meat, they still had not removed or destroyed the stone tablets. Another example would be the inner mountain of Koyasan, which was originally the monk's area for practice, and no woman was allowed to enter there. At the front of the mountain there was a structure with a sign that said, "Woman Stop" meaning that females must not enter. Although women were already having babies and raising children in the mountains, the "Woman Stop" structures were still there. Therefore, my Japanese friend who went with me said jokingly, "In the old times, woman must not enter. At the present time, women who entered were not allowed to come out." That was a joke, but it was a fact that they would not easily destroy or discard old monuments.

In terms of the monasteries of the Zen sect that specialized in holding Zen retreats, the lifestyle was still very rigid. Of course alcohol and meat were not allowed, least of all sexual affairs. Even if there were women, they were there to practice, not to be the wives of the monks. The Zen teachers of course had a family when they were in their youth and middle age, but after age 50-60, they would leave the family and live in the monasteries. They basically followed the practice of leading a life of purity. Their practice may appear to emphasize formality more than essence, but to a person new to the path, the restrictions on formality would be more important than the essential teachings of the mind. As a result, they were able to maintain the order relatively well and smoothly. The ordinary young monks would have to go through group practices two to four times, each time for one or two or even up to three months. Afterwards, they would appear differently in terms of their disposition, concept, faith, and manners. They would still get married and have children, drink alcohol and eat meat, but when they were in charge of ceremonies, socializing with the lay followers in various occasions, you would see them as well-mannered monks. They were also used to it and took it as normal. Japanese Buddhism, just the way it was, I could not say it was good, nor could I say it was bad. Of course it would be bad for the monks to live a conventional life, but you couldn't say that was wrong for lay people to take on religious duties and responsibilities after going through such training.

Generally speaking, traditional Japanese Buddhism, no matter which sect or school, would all pay much attention to the nurturing of future talents. If it were the eldest or a younger son that was appointed to succeed the abbot of the monastery, the abbot would make sure he trained the successor well. On one hand they could send them to the Buddhist department of the universities founded by various sects to complete the basic university degree, or at least take specialized training from the school's curriculum. On the other hand they could use the summer and winter vacation to send the successor to mountain monasteries of various sects for two or more periods of education through daily living practice, to enhance their faith, and to teach them demeanor. The process of the practice and training was very strict.

For example, the Minobusan of the Nichiren Sect had a special training for young people held in the winter. It was a kind of ascetic practice called *aragyo*, which began at 1 A.M. in the morning, under temperatures below zero degrees Celsius. The young monks would have to be naked, bare footed, with only shorts on; everyone would carry a water bucket, go to the well to fetch water, and then pour it from head to feet. They would pour 15-30 buckets of water consecutively. In the beginning, their teeth would chatter, and they would cry out loud, "Hoh! Hoh!" The mighty sound would echo through the valley. Although the well water had some warmth, but after it was fetched up to the ground, it would turn icy immediately. Therefore, after splashing oneself with the well water, the whole body would turn red. Yet strangely enough, the body did not turn purple and nobody caught a cold. This was how they trained their willpower and spirit of selflessness.

Once when I went there, they were training young people with this method. The abbot was sixty or more years old and wore thin clothes. He asked me whether I would like to give it a try, but after he saw me heavily wrapped up in my clothes, he shook his head and simply asked me to sit by the window and watch. I also participated in other winter Zen retreats held in Hokuriku, Japan. They ate very simple food—rice porridge with yellow pickled radish for breakfast, rice and miso soup with one small side dish for lunch. There were only snacks in the evening and no formal meals. According to the ordinary standards, it was not nutritious enough; especially in such a freezing winter, the calories were insufficient. What was even more interesting was that they slept at ten o'clock and got up at four in the morning; there were no heating facilities in the room, and at the corners outside the room were piles of snow at people's height. Luckily, there were two layers of wallpaper, so the cold wind outside would not enter the room directly. The mattress was a simple *tatami*, and the blanket was short and narrow. Although the blanket was thick enough, it could not allow the person to sleep lying down. Once one got into bed, one wouldn't dare move. If one was afraid of the cold, one could get up and do sitting meditation. In the first few days, I wanted to leave every day. I saw that none of the Japanese monks were leaving and thought it would be a shame for me, a Chinese monk, to leave. As a result, I endured it day by day, until I finally got used to it. I still liked that kind of method of practice.

One day, I told the master leading the retreat, "This place is so cold!" His reply was: "Didn't your Chinese patriarchs have a saying, 'Without enduring the chilling cold, how would you smell the fragrance of plum blossoms?'" I felt so ashamed. The Japanese used and followed through with the words of teachings of the Chinese patriarchs. However, the ancient Chinese Chan practitioners would live such a life everyday, every year, and for the whole life. The Zen practitioners in modern Japanese society would only come to participate in this way of living occasionally, so there was still a difference between them.

In Mainland China, in Shanghai where I once lived, there was an old monastery from the Six Dynasties (220-589), called the Jing'an Monastery. On April 8 of the lunar calendar each year, there would be a grand festival which would last for three days. Basically, other than things related to killing, the festival had almost everything—food, amusement, entertainment, show, and things that could be used. Such kinds of festival were quite popular in Mainland China. When I was in Tokyo, Japan, other than the New Year festivals at the Meiji Shrine and the Hachiman Shrine in Tokyo, I also had been to many large Buddhist festivals. One of the most lively events would be the Flower Festival held on April 8 by the Kodoshan Society in Yokohama. Actually, the festival was what in Taiwan we call the Buddha's Birthday Festival to commemorate the birth of Shakyamuni. They had a parade of all kinds of flowered floats to illustrate both in motion and still-life, stories of Buddhist history, including the so-called Eight Stages of the Complete Enlightenment from the life of the Buddha. They also had groups and groups of parades, with people wearing Japanese-style costumes from the different dynasties acting as pious Buddhists. The representatives from their Society came from their branches from various prefectures and cities, and they were divided into children, youth, middle-aged, elder, and the women's group.

The parade would last for three hours, and there was traffic control over the two streets for the whole period of time. The two sides of the street were full of people, and they were there to see the dynamic shows as well as the static exhibitions. Among the dynamic shows, they had bands, dancers, both traditional and modern. The most popular among Japanese people would be the traditional Japanese peasant dance. The men and women would wear white socks and white straw sandals, dressed in farm clothes that were bright in color, and wore decorated bamboo hats. They would dance as they walk; the style was beautiful and the music was also very pleasant. At the time, such a show had already become one of the major sightseeing events of the Yokohama District. It did have some effect on Buddhism in that anyone who visited would at least have the impression that Buddhist faith was popular among the people, and that it could be both solemn and conventional, and it was widely worshiped by Japanese society.

I also participated in the activities of the new religious groups, such as the National General Meeting of the Members of the Rissho Koseikai Society. The sight of the scene was even grander. Their head office was located in the Suginami District of Tokyo, and at the time they already utilized closed circuit television and big screens to make possible the meeting of tens of thousands of people in the same large building both indoors and outdoors. I was treated as their honored guest, and they appointed a high level supervisor to receive us, because the eldest son of their president Niwano Nikkyo was the appointed successor, and he was our classmate at Rissho University. They allowed us to take part in the entire meeting, and afterwards led us to visit the meeting room, guest room, and their kindergarten, elementary school, high school, and professional school.

They almost constructed their society as an independent kingdom. The fortunate followers were taken care of by their society from birth to death. They had many methods to attract, nurture, and care for their followers. One most coherent method would be the small group discussions known as the Dharma Seat. In every district and area they would use this method to communicate, following the methods taught by Niwano Nikkyo: the words distributed to them were used as the guideline for them to help each other; every one of them would speak their views or their difficulties and confusions. If they didn't have any difficulties, they could stand up and present an objective view, or what they had seen or heard through their own experience, to help the other members of the same group. Some of them knew each other and some of them met for the first time, but they would all interact like old friends. Under the care of the wisdom and compassion of Buddhism, they would help each other and take care of each other. Such a Dharma Seat was utilized in every district and area, and even during their National General Meeting.

That day after their president Niwano Nikkyo gave a short speech, the members were divided into groups according to their districts, forming many small groups of ten to eight people. The groups would sit down and discuss animatedly. Within their group the more senior members would know how to answer all the questions of the newcomers through their own personal experiences, and from the lecture materials issued by the Rissho Koseikai Society. There were also higher members to assist the president. Therefore, there were only very few questions that the president would be required to answer in person himself. This kind of event allowed all the participating members to feel much fulfilled, and they would return home full of joy.

I also participated in the Japanese Buddhist ceremonies for redeeming the dead, which they called Hoyo, a memorial service. The concept was similar to the Chinese belief that reciting the sutras could help redeem the souls of the dead and allow them to become a buddha sooner. They would usually read the large sutras such as the *Lotus Sutra* or *Avatamsaka Sutra*. What was clever was they would only read one chapter or one section of the sutra as if it were the whole sutra. Nevertheless, the whole sutra would be put on the table, and after reading one chapter they would open up the remaining unread sections, and then flip through the rest of the pages as if pulling an accordion. They would do this for all the remaining unread volumes and counted that as if they had read through them. If this happened in China, the donors who paid for the monks and nuns to recite the sutras would complain, "That's called cheating the ghosts!" However, in Japan that was just normal custom.

Since Japanese Buddhism originated in China, I initially thought that their monasteries would use the same sutras and texts of repentance as those we had in China. However, I later discovered that they were quite different; they didn't have the Liang Emperor Repentance, the Samadhi Water Repentance, the Great Compassion Repentance, or the Amitabha Repentance. As for the ceremony of offering food to the hungry ghosts, it was even more unheard of; the reason being that these things were gradually formed after the Song Dynasty in China, and the establishment of the ceremony for offerings to the hungry ghosts happened even later in the late Ming Dynasty. Japanese Buddhism absorbed the format of Chinese Buddhism from the Sui (581-618), Tang, and Song dynasties, so they didn't have these things. For example, every year in July, they would also have the Hungry Ghost Festival, also known as the Ullambana Festival. However, in Japan, they would recite the *Lotus Sutra* or *Diamond Sutra* or other Pure Land sutras translated from India or even the textbooks compiled by their own patriarchs. This made me realize that the current Chinese Buddhism was not the same Chinese Buddhism learned by the Japanese. The Chinese Buddhism brought back by the Japanese was not the kind of Chinese Buddhism modern people had in mind. The Chinese people often said that the Japanese forgot their roots, that they forgot about the Chinese people, and used their own things and developed their own style of Buddhism. However, that was actually a normal phenomenon, because even the modern Chinese people forgot about the original face of Chinese Buddhism from the Sui, Tang and Song dynasties.

Writing While not Attending to Proper Duties

When I was studying in Japan I didn't have a fixed sponsor, so I was concerned about having money for food and tuition. As a result, in the first few years I would recite sutras or speak the Dharma for the Chinese people in Japan. Although the pay was limited, it was better than nothing, and better than taking off the monk's robes and working in the restaurants. Occasionally some Chinese Buddhists from Southeast Asia would visit Japan, and I could earn some fees by being their tour guide. Although they were quite polite, treating me as a monk and offering me money, it was also a fact that I did tour guiding for them. Since I was constantly troubled by financial problems and could be forced to end my student life abroad at any time, I hoped to quickly learn and absorb the various current aspects of Japanese Buddhism, and reported them back to Taiwan as soon as possible. In my mind, letting people in Taiwan gain more understanding of Japanese Buddhism would be of some help to the Buddhism in Taiwan. At the time Taiwan was still an underdeveloped country while Japan had already become a world-leading economic and cultural nation. The Chinese monks in ancient times traveled to India to retrieve the sutras and learn from them to help grow and nurture Chinese culture. I came to Japan and didn't retrieve any new sutras, but I hoped to at least bring back some new experience to facilitate the new development of the Buddhist culture in Taiwan.

With such intention and ideology when I was in Japan, I started writing down what I saw and heard before fully understanding Japanese, and mailed my impressions to Taiwan to be published in Buddhist magazines. A famous work written by Master Faxian (ca. 337-422) after his travel to India was *The Record of Buddhist Countries*, and Master Xuanzang (ca. 602-664) wrote the *Great Tang*

Records on the Western Regions after his travel to India. Master Yijing who studied abroad in the Western Regions sent back by sea his work *The Account of Buddhism Sent from the Southern Seas*. In the past, there were many monks and lay people who studied in Japan, but few of them introduced the modern Japan. As a result, people who had been to Japan would sympathize with them, while the people who had not been to Japan would misunderstand them. Those who returned after studying abroad, due to their sympathy with Japan, would be called "foreigner's slaves," "boot-lickers for Japan," and "Chinese traitors." This was actually caused by the opposition between both parties due to the estrangement from each other.

As a result, when I arrived in Japan, I recorded what I saw or heard with a more objective attitude and wrote down their strengths to report them back to Taiwan. I was not advocating for the Japanese, I was just hoping to learn something from them. The so-called, "the stone on the other mountain can be the grindstone to sharpen our knife (someone else has something worth learning)." As a result, besides studying diligently to complete all the school homework and working very hard on completing the theses for my degrees, I also used as much spare time as possible to collect resource materials to write articles to send to Taiwan. During one period of time, it was a very important stage in writing my theses, but I would still not attend to my proper duties and wrote articles that were unrelated to my thesis. Six years later when I left Tokyo, I collected the various magazines in Taiwan, and found that I had written articles on Japan for over 300,000 words. Therefore, in 1979, I compiled them into a book named *From East to West* (Chn. *Congdongyang daoxiyang*)and published it in Taiwan.

The book was divided into five sections, with a total of thirty-three articles. Twenty six articles I wrote in Japan, including "Reports on Studying Abroad," "Critiques on Japanese Buddhism," "Buddhist History," "Memorial for the Teachers," "Buddhist Concepts," etc. In the "Reports" I told of my life, my views, and events that happened around me, as well as what happened in Japan during the period I studied in Japan. As for the "Critiques" on Japanese Buddhism, they were actually the reports and explanations of what I saw on Japanese Buddhism. For example, the academic Buddhism, the lay Buddhism, and the historical directions of Buddhism, the international Buddhism in Japan, the monastic Buddhism, and the Buddhism in universities, as well as the Buddhism of the new religious cults.

The "Buddhist History" actually revolves around the ripple effect on the academic community of Japanese Buddhism of Master Yinshun's *History of Chinese Chan*. I wrote three articles: first, a review of the book in three parts, published in the *Shanghainese China Foreign Daily*, and which was translated into Japanese. I wrote another article about my feelings on the process of Master Yinshun's attainment of the Doctorate in Literature from Rissho University, and I published it in the *Bodhi Tree* magazine in Taiwan. Another article was written for the first International Buddhist History Conference in 1976. It discussed four Buddhist philosophers: Master Ouyi from the late Ming Dynasty, and three contemporary masters: Master Taixu, Master Yinshun, and Layman Ouyang Jingwu. My purpose was still to introduce Master Yinshun to the Buddhist academic communities worldwide in that we had such a philosopher in modern-day China. It was published in the second year after I went to America, but the constitution and formation of its ideology were implemented when I was in Japan.

In addition, during the time I was studying for my doctorate courses, my advisor Prof. Sakamoto Yukio suddenly passed away. This caused me much grief and I wrote a long article in memorial for him. During this same time, on invitation from *Neiming* magazine in Hong Kong to submit articles, I translated into Chinese one of my reading reports, "The Tiantai Thought of Three Thousand Worlds Immanent in an Instant of One Thought." In the foreword of that article, I made a declaration to reflect my thoughts and attitudes at the time: "The article was one of the Japanese research papers I wrote last year, when I was studying my first year doctorate courses. Prior to this, I wasn't an expert on researching Tiantai. In terms of the content of this article, it was an organization and introduction on the history of scholastic thought, and it was mainly based on the research results of the modern Japanese Buddhist scholars. However, it was still new to the Chinese Buddhist community, so I translated it into Chinese, and provided it to the readers and editors of *Neiming* magazine for comments and corrections."

In the 70's, the people in the Chinese Buddhist community who could write articles and books mostly still followed the traditional way of study. For example, when they quoted from the sutras, they would only tell you that a certain sutra or shastra said this and that, but they wouldn't indicate the chapters, and surely not the page numbers. If they quoted from the views of modern people, they would only tell you that a certain person said this, but very few people would tell you which book the quote was from, and certainly would not footnote on the page number. They were also too lazy to use quotation marks, and would let the readers figure out themselves sections that were quoted from other people's words and the parts that were the author's own opinions. This was because they were used to the classical works, which were all like this. The most outstanding thinker in modern

China, Master Yinshun, was also not an exception. Not until he had accepted the opinions for taking on the modern ways of study and research did he complete the *History of Chinese Chan* and that was in the 70's. Afterwards, the works of Master Yinshun all met the common formats and ways of expression of international academic community standards.

The Academic Conferences of Japanese Buddhism
When I decided to study in Japan, my friends who were currently studying there, or who had completed their studies and returned, were all very eager to provide me with many suggestions. Those from Kyoto would tell you that if you wanted to learn the genuine and steadfast Japanese culture, it would be best to go to Kyoto. It would allow you to review the ancient style of study in the Chinese Tang and Song dynasties. An accomplished scholar would only focus on one subject within his lifetime; he would become the most authoritative scholar in this field, and he would have the habit of passing it down from father to son, master to pupil. If you were in Kyoto and could learn from a master-grade scholar, and you worked hard with diligence, the scholar would promote you, and you would become his descendant. Therefore, the style of the Kyoto school of studies was very rigid.

On the other hand, the friends in Tokyo would emphasize that the center of contemporary Japanese culture is not Kyoto, but Tokyo. Tokyo is not only the center of Japanese culture but also one of the important distribution centers in today's world culture. Only in Tokyo could one sense the dynamics of the academic culture of Japanese Buddhism, and could breathe the fresh air of the academic research atmosphere of world Buddhism. Many world-class and international academic conferences were mainly held in Tokyo. Even if one may not have any works to present, one could still get a sense of academic atmosphere from simply attending these conferences and listen and watch.

The result was that I went to Tokyo, not because I listened to the suggestions of any of my friends, but because in Kyoto I had nobody to act as my guarantor. I didn't know any Chinese who had the residence status, and the students studying abroad didn't have the residence status, so they were not qualified. Mr. Zhang Mantao once tried to find ways for me by asking his advising professor at Otani University, and he also sent him a set of my published books. The professor was quite polite but I didn't hear from him afterwards. However, Master Huiyue who just returned to Taiwan after completing his studies at Rissho University in Tokyo, Japan promised to complete the procedures for me. At the same time, there was a Mr. Wu Laoze who just came back from his vacation, so I asked him to help me. I handed him my personal information as well as Master Huiyue's letter of recommendation, and he found Master Huiyue's advisor, Prof. Sakamoto Yukio. It was really very simple. The procedures were completed very quickly, and I received the letter of acceptance for admission from Tokyo. It was not my choice that I went to Tokyo but the result of causes and conditions.

In the Japanese Buddhist academic community the competition was quite fierce, and the divisions between the schools were also quite evident. If one were not a genuine talent with solid learning, there was no place for him in the academic and educational community. As a result, once one enters their university's master courses—which we called the institute's master program—if one wished to have a seat in their academic community in the future, one must work diligently with full effort. Not only had one to share the administrative work, one also needed to study hard and work for opportunities to present the thesis papers. If one could write, there was no need to worry about having a place to present them. If one's writing skills were poor, then don't even think about having the opportunity to present. There were many large and small academic conferences in the Japanese Buddhist academic community. Some of them were held by the home-school, and some of them were national Japanese Buddhist conferences.

For example, the Buddhist Department of Rissho University itself and the Nichiren Sect Department each had their own conference and school journal. The full name of the journal was *Osaki Gakuho* (*Journal of Nichiren and Buddhist Studies*) because Rissho University was located near the Osaki station in Shinagawa district, Tokyo. I was their member as of right, and had published several articles. The nationwide conference includes The Nippon Buddhist Research Association, and the mono-themed conferences include Japanese Association for Tibetan Studies and Japanese Association for Religious Studies, which was also called the Japanese Association for the Study of Taoism. I was a member of all of them. The largest, the one with the most people and the largest scope, was the Japanese Association of Indian and Buddhist Studies. If you often participated in all kinds of academic conferences, you would often meet those master-grade scholars in the conference as well as the later-risen new scholars. If you presented your theses very often and your works had good content and reason, then after the conference you would be able to publish it in their journal, the *Journal of Indian and Buddhist Studies*. You would also be recognized as one of their familiar scholars.

If a scholar completed a thesis for the doctoral degree, but the academic community never heard of his or her name, this would be one with no name and no reputation. No matter how well the thesis was written, there was not much probability for it to be passed. For more than six years in Japan, I participated in various conferences, from small ones to large ones of several hundred people and attended over twenty of them. The purpose was to listen to other people's presentations and to show my face to others, and let others know about my existence. It was not a problem if one did not present any thesis and simply went there to listen to other people's opinions. It was also not a shame if the theses one presented in the conferences were not selected for publishing. It would be nice for people to know you cared about academics, and were diligently doing research. I was such a person—I would go to the conferences but was unable to write something, and I would present thesis papers but not get them published. Actually, to be a scholar in Japan you must let people have a solid impression that you were doing research on a certain text, in a certain specialized field or subject. Every time you wrote a thesis, it should correspond with the topic of the doctoral thesis you were currently working on. However, you could not present any part of the doctoral thesis itself. Otherwise, that thesis would not be passed.

While studying for the doctoral courses, my thesis topic was on Master Ouyi. Therefore, between 1973 and 1974, all the theses I presented were related to Master Ouyi. My doctoral thesis was passed in 1975. Therefore, although the two articles presented in the conference of the Japanese Association of Indian and Buddhist Studies were just byproducts of my main subject, they were written to academic standards. As a result, they were published in issues No.43 and No.45 of the *Journal of Indian and Buddhist Studies* respectively. Their titles were "The Ancestral List of Characters in the Works of Master Zhixu and Master Zhixu's Thoughts" and "Study of Tiantai."

In order to attend the various academic conferences, I traveled to many places in Japan. Since they were the academic conferences within the sect or school, the various major monasteries would take turns providing the venue and funding for the conferences. As for the national conferences, the related universities of the participating organizational members would organize them. If a scholar attended the conference as an individual, he or she would become an individual member. The institutes that participated in the conferences under the name of the school would become an organizational member. If the institute of the organizational members had a Buddhist department, they surely had some professors doing Buddhist research. They would estimate the manpower and financial power to take turns in organizing the conferences.

I often traveled with Japanese classmates to the various conferences, and didn't need to worry about anything besides paying for long distance carfare. Classmates of Rissho University have acquaintances almost everywhere. There were a total of around 80,000 monasteries in Japan. Therefore, we could find monasteries to stay at overnight that would provide us food and drinks. Or we would stay in the homes of the classmates' friends, and accept their hospitality for food and accommodations, as well as transportation. Due to this reason, besides Shikoku, which I had not been to, I went south to Okinawa, north to Hokkaido, and I visited almost every prefecture. However, I went to the areas around Tokyo more frequently. It was better to stay in the Japanese monasteries than the hotels. Regardless of the size of the monasteries, their places were all clean and tidy, and the people were very kind and friendly. It was most thoughtful that they considered providing me with vegetarian cuisine.

Among the Japanese graduate students working for the master's degree, some had no plan to become a scholar and only wanted the honor of having studied in the university. However, there were also many who studied very diligently; they completed their thesis long before they would attend the academic conference, and handed it to their advising professor for proofreading again and again. They would prepare for the conference in the car on their way to the conference. When they checked in for accommodations, they would wake up early and stayed up late to prepare for their presentation. This was similar to the pupils in the ancient Chinese tutorage schools, who would read the books out loud before they memorized it early in the morning. They would read their papers out loud, in fear of stage fright or not being able to read them smoothly or even going overtime in their presentations. This kind of spirit of striving for excellence was really moving.

Chapter 8

My Doctor's Thesis

Academics and Faith

I did not have the orientation and temperament of a scholar, nor did I plan to become a scholar when I was young. I was diligent in my studies and writings but that was not my purpose. The proverb says: "As for the joy of reading, one can find beauty as good as jade in books; in the joy of reading one can also find among books a house of treasure." I didn't find reading particularly joyful, was not addicted to reading, nor did I have the habit of reading as a must. I didn't think about escaping from reality in books, or enjoying visions of beauty as good as jade and a house of treasure in books. Of course I wouldn't think about using the knowledge from reading to get myself a wife and buy houses. Contrarily, I didn't find reading particularly painful either. The sense of loss from the so-called "ten years of oblivion in school" never happened. As a result, for me, I could read or not read.

Why did the ancient Chinese scholars advocate reading the books of saints and sages? It was a wish to equal the saints and sages and a dedication to emulate those who are wise and virtuous, which was why Han Yu advocated "Writings are for conveying the truth." Since I read Buddhist texts, I knew that language, words, and terms were all unrelated to the matter of [the cycle of] birth and death. The first chapter of the *Mahaprajnaparamita Shastra* said: "Truth exceeds all language and sayings," which means that what can be conveyed by words and language were not all the truth. That was why the Chan school advocated "not giving rise to words and language." The Patriarch Bodhidharma said, "Do not be led by words and teachings." The *Platform Sutra* of Huineng advocates no relying on words. Therefore, the Confucian dictum, "Compared to everything else there is nothing better than reading" did not mean much to me.

Before going to Japan I had already read and written many books. I had only one reason and purpose in mind: to absorb the knowledge from those books and share that with everyone. I wanted to share the benefits rather than the knowledge itself and to inform those who should know and didn't know, so *they* could know. For those who didn't know and misunderstood, I tried to help them understand; for those who understood but didn't know how to use the knowledge, I would show them the ways and methods. I didn't dare use my own personal opinions and force them onto others, and I always wanted to use Buddhist concepts to help others.

When I wrote my master's thesis, I always thought that the book *The Mahayana Shamatha-Vipashyana Practice* [by Master Huisi] was both intellectual and implemental. After I completed my thesis, I realized that it was a philosophical and theoretical book. Its purpose was to let people accept that the Tathagatagarbha concept was correct, so people could establish the faith that everyone could become a buddha. That book had been published for over ten years and many people bought it thinking that they would find the methods of practice in it. However, they realized that they were fooled after they read through it, because the book was not about practice, but theory and research. I felt very sorry for this. However, since it was a book of research, it allowed me to be granted my master's degree, so I should feel grateful towards the author.

Even though the master's degree was useless to me personally, I could still use it to contribute to the cause of Buddhism. Without it, I would not be able to enter the doctoral degree program. And if I didn't have a doctorate, I would not have the status recognized by the academic and education communities, and not be able to receive related posts. Without the degrees, I wouldn't have the qualifications and the ability to personally establish higher education and nurture high grade talents. To become a successful coach of a swimming team one should at least be able to swim; or if a sports team, play that sport. I was therefore compelled by causes and conditions to take the master's and doctoral degree courses, as well as write both theses.

I was involved in academics and research for my faith, rather than for their own sake. For example, why did I choose Master Ouyi Zhixu as the subject for my doctoral thesis? It was for three reasons: first, Master Ouyi was one of the four great masters of the late Ming Dynasty, not only a scholar but a practitioner, a true believer of the so-called "unity of practice and knowledge," which was the principal guideline of Buddhadharma. Second, people recognized Master Ouyi as the last great achiever of the Chinese Tiantai school. I yearned for what the Tiantai school advocated as equal emphasis on teaching and meditation, and the simultaneous functioning of shamatha (calming) and vipashyana (contemplation). The reason is that the equal emphasis on concepts and meditation practice is exactly the spirit required by Buddhism today. And finally, when I asked my advisor Prof. Sakamoto Yukio for his opinion on this choice of topic, he said that he originally planned to write on it himself but he was old now, and had not heard from another Chinese student studying abroad whom he once encouraged to write on it. Therefore, he said it would be great if I would be willing to write on this topic.

I asked him, "What should I write about?" He said, "Master

Ouyi Zhixu. Everyone said he was a great master of the Tiantai school. What exactly did he say? He had many works that all seem complicated and this required research." He said, "During the same time in the Edo period in Japan, there was a Tendai scholar named Reiku Koken (1652-1739). In his *Preface of the Carving of Master Ouyi's Discussions on the Essence of the Dharma* (Chn. *Lingfeng zonglun*), he said, 'Anyone who read Master Ouyi's *Discussions on the Essence of the Dharma* and not fall into tears must be one who had not given rise to bodhi-mind.'" I had not yet read *Discussions on the Essence of the Dharma* but I thought that if people could be moved to tears and give rise to bodhi-mind after reading it then it must be a good book, and modern Buddhists must have an urgent need to know about it. As a result I decided on that as my doctoral thesis topic.

This happened in the spring of 1972, and from then I began collecting resource materials for the thesis. In order to express my gratitude to the Buddha, I should spread the spirit of Master Ouyi. Prof. Sakamoto was a scholar and also a Buddhist with firm faith, and that was why he cared about research on Master Ouyi. When I completed my master's I had no financial backing, and I was about to pack my luggage and return to my home country. When I told Prof. Sakamoto about my difficulties he quoted two lines from Reiku Koken: "There is food and clothing within the mind of the Dharma, but there is no bodhi-mind in food and clothing." He urged me to work for the Dharma and not worry about having no support for livelihood, and that I should nourish the spirit of seeking the Dharma amidst hardship and difficulties. This kind of encouragement was what I needed the most at the time, and it was even more useful than being promised financial support.

After one semester in the summer of 1970, an anonymous

benefactor wrote from Switzerland and promised to support my expenditures for studying abroad. However, due to the depreciation of the US dollar, the fund I applied for was insufficient. When Prof. Sakamoto learned about this, he said he hoped I could submit my doctoral thesis before the spring of 1975, prior to his retirement. As for the expenditures, he would help me out with a donation of between 600,000-800,000 Japanese Yen per year. Luckily, the benefactor from Switzerland made a second remittance, and made up for the remaining insufficient amount. Unfortunately, in 1973 Prof. Sakamoto passed away and my doctoral thesis had still not been completed or submitted. Although funding was no longer a problem, there was a problem with the advisor for my thesis. I could only silently pray in my heart hoping that I could pass through this difficulty. In the end two old friends of Prof. Sakamoto's—Prof. Kanakura Ensho and Prof. Nomura Yosho—took on the job, and they became my chief advisor and vice advisor. As a result, my doctoral thesis was attained through the support of faith.

Difficulties in Resource Material Collection

Master Ouyi's works were mainly collected in the *Manji Zokuzokyo (Xuzangjing) Tripitaka*, and there were two works that were collected in the *Taisho Tripitaka*. From these works, I discovered the titles of his other related writings. I hoped to collect all of his works but didn't know where they were, and I didn't know where I should start. Although they already had computer facilities in Japan, the libraries were not yet so advanced that you could get the list of all the works and their locations simply by entering the name "Master Ouyi Zhixu." Master Ouyi's works, with different content and written in different eras, would have different signatures. Therefore, it was very difficult to collect all the information. Luckily, I had my own simple method, which was not to wait until all the resource materials were collected before commencing research and writing. I would write as I read and as I researched.

In Japan many people knew about Master Ouyi, and also many people used Master Ouyi's materials, especially his works *Entry into the Tripitaka* (Chn. *Yuezang zhijin*) and *Essential Guidelines for Teaching and Contemplation* (Chn. *Jiaoguan gangzong*) and his literary collection *Discussions on the Essence of the Dharma*. If one wanted to find published research theses that were genuine research and introductions on Master Ouyi, there were very few and they did not propose much opinion. This allowed me to be at ease, put them all aside and just focus my research on the works of Master Ouyi. At the same time, for this reason I found it especially difficult to start my work. With no tracks or clues to trace, I did not know where to begin. Master Ouyi paid special attention to bibliography. However, there was no bibliography for his own works, and nobody after him had organized it for him.

The works of Master Ouyi were large and complex in scope. He was a master well versed in Buddhist studies, as well as a thoroughly studied master in Confucianism. He was even involved in the discussion and criticism of Christianity. Therefore, it seemed that those works that were totally unrelated to Buddhism were not collected in the *Tripitaka*. Some of his works were republished by later generations and were given different titles; their contents added to, deleted, and edited. I had to collect them all and compare them word-by-word to distinguish their sequence, and that took a lot of time and effort. Over two years' time I had gradually identified Master Ouyi's works that were left out by the *Tripitaka*.

One of Master Ouyi's most important works consists of the texts that make up the *Discussions on the Essence of the Dharma*. After he passed away, the work was compiled, published and distributed by his monastic disciple, Master Chengshi. In Master Chengshi's preface to the *Discussions on the Essence of the Dharma* he said: "Aside from the commentaries, there were seven manuscripts compiled into one book. The works were grouped into categories. The other works that were originally excluded from the manuscripts were also collected, and there were a total of ten main chapters, sub-divided into thirty-eight sub-chapters." The compiler did not inform us of the original names of the seven manuscripts, but they could be seen spread out among Master Ouyi's works. The reason was because the compiler had spread them apart and also added in articles besides the manuscripts. However, as far as I was concerned, I had to search out the original titles and contents of those seven manuscripts in order to discover the paragraphs and arrangement of ideas of Master Ouyi's works. Since these seven independent articles were once published individually, where were they now?

Actually, when I initially began to search for Master Ouyi's works, I only had a copy of *The Chronicle of Master Ouyi's Life* compiled by Master Hongyi. It was a very short booklet, printed in Font Size 4, page layout 32, with a total of 29 pages. The resource information Master Hongyi could obtain at the time was not complete; therefore, it was not compiled in detail. However, it was like a treasure for me at the time. I never saw the most important work *Discussions on the Essence of the Dharma*. Before I went abroad, I heard that a certain master in southern Taiwan had collected such a book, and he was a very familiar friend of mine. I wrote to him and requested to borrow it from him. I wrote two letters, and there were no replies. Perhaps

I wrote the wrong address or perhaps he was worried that he might never get it back after mailing such a precious ancient text to Japan. When I met him and asked him about this afterwards, he only smiled and did not reply. I had already completed the thesis and obtained the degree at the time.

Searching for this book from catalogs at libraries of various universities, my efforts were in vain. As a last resort I could only ask my advisor Prof. Sakamoto; I believed he must have seen it or knew where to find it. Luckily, he just stepped on a chair, and from the top of his bookshelf he took down a set of string-bound texts. It was an eighteenth-century wooden block edition reprint in Japan. The cover was wrapped with painted paper, with a total of ten volumes, and on every volume there was the book title written in formal Chinese calligraphy in black ink on a white background, in block letters, the words "*Master Ouyi's Discussions on the Essence of the Dharma.*" Prof. Sakamoto lent the texts to me on condition that I only read them and not make any markings on them, and that I must return them within a month. I treated the texts as an invaluable treasure that I had found and replied to the professor: "No problem! I will return them within a week!" He knew what I was going to do and said: "It would be best to photocopy a set!" As a result, I used *Discussions on the Essence of the Dharma* as the center and source of clues for my research, and read it over 27 times within 2 years.

There were a total of 51 texts and 228 chapters of Master Ouyi's works. Those works that the common people thought were important could be found in the *Tripitaka*; therefore, they were not so important to me in terms of collecting resource materials. On the other hand, those works that were ignored by later generations became very important to me. First, I made a bibliography of the titles of all of

Master Ouyi's writings that were mentioned in his works. Then, from the related information from Master Ouyi's works, I would discover the different pen names used by him, and then try to find his other works based on his pen name. The best reference was that every time he wrote a book, there must be a preface, an origin, and a postscript, which would mention the names of a few related works. I went to various university libraries in Tokyo and its surrounding areas to search for them, or asked friends in Kyoto to search for me in the libraries of several Buddhist related universities.

In the end I was able to obtain the photocopies of all of them. For example, I found that *Collected Essays Refuting Heterodoxy* (Chn. *Pixie ji*) and *An Interpretation of Book of Changes from the Perspective of Chan Buddhism* (Chn. *Zhouyi chanjie*) were collected by the Komazawa University in Tokyo. I found *Observing the Waves of the Dharma Sea* (Chn. *Fahai guanlan*) collected by the Taisho University in Tokyo. I found *Chart of Selecting the Buddhas* (Chn. *Xuanfo pu*) collected by the Ryukoku University in Kyoto. I couldn't find the book *Explanation of the Four Books* (Chn. *Sishu ouyi jie*) anywhere, and yet in 1973 after I returned to Taiwan, I found a printed copy of it published by Taiwan Sage Publisher on a bookstand along the streets in Taipei. It's a pity that the book left out *Mencius Selecting Milk* (Chn. *Mengzi zeru*).

Later, I also discovered five of the single-volume editions of the seven original literary works that were compiled into *Discussions on the Essence of the Dharma*: (1) *The Q&A at the Hall of Pure Faith* (Chn. *Jingxintang dawen*), three chapters, collected by the Philosophy Department of Toyo University in Tokyo; (2) *Three Verses of Master Ouyi* (Chn. *Ouyi's sansong*), one chapter, collected by Komazawa University in the *Ming Edition Tripitaka's Further Addition Version—* Set No.48, Book No.8; (3) *Occasional Talk in the Dharma Room*

(Chn. *Fanshi outan*); (4) *Dawning on the Study of the Nature of the Mind* (Chn. *Xingxue kaimeng*) also collected in Komazawa University in the *Ming Edition Tripitaka's Further Addition Version*—Set No.80, Book No.9; (5) *Ending the Residuals* (Chn. *Jueyu pian*), collected in Komazawa University.

I compared the content of these five single volume edition ancient texts with the content of *Discussions on the Essence of the Dharma*, and discovered that there were many differences between them. Basically, compared to the original texts, *Discussions on the Essence of the Dharma* was a much-simplified edited version. However, it was unknown whether the editing was done by the hands of Master Ouyi or if it was the doing of the compiler Master Chengshi. Not only that, in the earlier single volume edition, Master Ouyi would list the names of the monastic and lay disciples whom he met, saw, or thought about in detail, but in *Discussions on the Essence of the Dharma* only a few names that were frequently mentioned were left.

One needed to be persistent and never stop in midway or shrink back from difficulties in the process of collecting writing materials. The Japanese culture placed much importance on the collection of resource materials. When their scholars visited China and heard or saw which place had ancient texts, they would collect them back to Japan no matter whether they were useful to them or not. The ancient Buddhist scriptures one could find in China were very limited. However, in Japan, they already compiled several sets of *Tripitaka*, and they also categorized all the ancient Chinese Buddhist texts they collected from ancient times to the present time, and compiled them into books. There were still many available materials that were not compiled into the *Tripitaka*. Therefore, I was very confident that I could find all the texts of Master Ouyi which were only 320 years away from the time I wrote this thesis, and were once published somewhere in Japan.

Master Hongyi mentioned in *The Chronicle of Master Ouyi's Life* (collected in *The Bibliography*, Text 1, of *The Collection of Master Ouyi*, Taipei: Buddhist Publishers, 1989) that there were only 47 works of Master Ouyi. However, I saw 51 of them and Master Hongyi probably didn't actually see the content of the 47 works mentioned in *The Chronicle of Master Ouyi's Life* because it was impossible to find them all in China.

Chinese people like simple and practical things. The skills of "diving into the sea and counting sand" were actually quite meaningless to them. Until the present day, some of them would still say that the Japanese or Western scholars doing research on Buddhist studies were only "plucking chicken feathers and peeling garlic" (doing superficial work) and "counting beans and sand" (not very useful). They commented that scholars only knew about collecting, comparing, compiling, and introducing the materials, and that they would write a book which would be stacked on a bookshelf. That it was of no use to living real life or encouraging practice. Its only use was that future scholars could use their materials and write another book which was boring! It sounded like they made sense. The proverb says "study for the purpose of application," meaning that studying was for the purpose of benefiting the world. In the end I spent six years studying in Japan using this kind of method and skills. I spent much time on writing my thesis but very few people were interested in reading it. However, the value of this kind of book was not on its distribution but on the clarification of issues. Although there was only one copy of the book, it would become a record, setting the course of history.

Discoveries through Thesis Writing

From Master Ouyi's autobiography, we see that he cast four [divining] lots to ask the Buddha which school he should specialize in: the Huayan Xianshou, the Fahua Tiantai, or the Faxiang Ci'en, or establish a new school. In other words, whether he should specialize in a particular school or establish his own to expound the Buddhadharma. The result was that for several times, he kept picking up the lot of Fahua Tiantai school. Therefore, afterwards he explained the sutras and shastras according to the Tiantai method for making commentaries. He also wrote an essential book on the Tiantai school, *Essential Guidelines for Teaching and Contemplation*, and a commentary on the *Lotus Sutra*, the *Summary on the Meaning of Lotus Sutra* (Chn. *Fahua huiyi*), and a book on the central concepts of Tiantai school, *Abstract of the Essential Meaning of Lotus Sutra* (Chn. *Fahua xuanyi jieyao*).

As a result he was recognized by later generations as a great thinker of the Tiantai school. If one wanted to understand Master Ouyi, one would have to understand the teachings of the Tiantai school first. As a result I started reading Master Zhiyi's (538-597) *Essential Sayings of Lotus Sutra* (Chn. *Fahua wenju*), *Essential Meaning of Lotus Sutra* (Chn. *Fahua xuanyi*), and *The Great Calming and Contemplation* (Chn. *Mohe zhiguan*). At the time, I was hoping to research Master Ouyi's works through the philosophical patterns of the Tiantai school. As a result I tried to compare Master Ouyi's *Summary on the Meaning of Lotus Sutra* and *Abstract of the Essential Meaning of Lotus Sutra* with Master Zhiyi's works. I didn't have any new discoveries, so I had to give up my efforts in this direction. I then discovered that the scope of his works was very wide and didn't know where [within this scope] to begin my writing. If I only attempted to discuss Master Ouyi's

Ouyi's thoughts from the point of view of one sutra or shastra that would not fully cover it. Therefore, I decided to organize his works chronologically, to decipher his tracks, thoughts, the period his works were completed in, and the location where they were written, as well as the people he had contact with. Only then could I have a clear and full view of Master Ouyi's entire life, including his studies, writing, practice, relationships, and the origin of his thoughts and its changes.

The first chapter of the thesis dealt with the history of Master Ouyi's time. From his works one could discover the conditions of society, politics, academia , and religion of his time. I would then use what he had seen or heard as the clues, and focus on that to collect the related auxiliary materials and historical facts. In this way, the thesis would allow us to feel as if we were on the spot, personally experiencing the environment of Master Ouyi's period. It was during the late Ming when the dynasty was in decline and in chaos; society was unstable, and the neo-Confucians were attacking Buddhism. It was a time of turmoil when there was a prevailing advocacy of the concept of "the same origin of the three faiths" (Confucianism, Buddhism, and Taoism); the wide spreading of Christianity and its competition with Buddhism, as well as the decay of the Buddhist sangha.

In the second chapter I wrote on Master Ouyi's life, including the lineage of his master, the people he admired, allies, friends, and disciples. I analyzed the materials on Master Ouyi's biography to determine, research, and introduce the geography of his whereabouts. I also discovered when and where, and whom he was with, for what reason, and what actually happened.

Chapter 3 was about the faith and practice of Master Ouyi. This section was mainly based on the information in *Discussions on the*

Essence of the Dharma. He was a person with very strong religious faith and very firm determination; one could also say that he was a very sensitive person. He was ill most of his life, so he believed he was a person with heavy karmic retribution and demonic obstructions. He was constantly engaged in introspection, and was self-demanding, and self-criticizing. He didn't believe that he could be able to practice successfully, eliminate karmic obstructions, and gain liberation from life and death with his own powers. He believed that he must rely on the powers of the buddhas and bodhisattvas and their compassionate salvation. He also believed that in order to receive a response from the buddhas and bodhisattvas, one must work hard and practice various activities diligently.

He believed in the compassionate empowerment of Avalokiteshvara (Guanyin) Bodhisattva and Kshitigarbha (Earth Treasury) Bodhisattva; he also strongly wished for guidance from Amitabha Buddha. In his youth he had a few spiritual experiences which he thought were enlightenment, but afterwards those experiences did not result in any actual benefit in his ability to master [the issue of] life-and-death. Therefore, his whole life he did repentance, mantra recitation, writing sutras with his blood, and burning his arms and head as dedication to the buddhas. In the end he solely wished for the guidance from Amitabha to be reborn in the Western Pure Land. Although he read many records of sayings from the Chan school, he still selected Amitabha's Western Pure Land as his ultimate refuge. Therefore, he had a work, *The Essentials of the Amitabha Sutra*, which was written quite well and has received popular acceptance even up to the present.

Chapter 4 was about the works of Master Ouyi. He advocated "knowing before practice," which means that knowledge and understanding of Buddhadharma were essential requirements for practicing Buddhadharma. Of his many works, all emphasized several concepts: consistency in the theories and methods of practice, dual learning of teaching and meditation, correspondence between understanding and realization, and the inseparable nature of faith, understanding and practice. Regarding his attitude in writing, he was very rigid. He emphasized both evidence and creativity, and he proposed "learning from the strengths of others and experiencing enlightenment with one's mind." He disliked the works of the other scholars of the time and thought that they were "forced interpretations with no foundation."

My introduction to Master Ouyi's works was done by using the concept of bibliography. I used the method of chronicles and compiled his works into a list of contents. I then noted the number of chapters, where they were written, their current location, and the signature he used. After I organized them into tables, it appeared to be clear and simple. Within his works, nineteen weren't marked with the actual date when they were written. However, according to their content and the evolution in Master Ouyi's thoughts, one could still infer the time they were written.

From the sequence of his works, one finds that between ages 30 to 40, Master Ouyi emphasized the *Vinaya* of both Hinayana and Mahayana. After age forty he wrote commentaries on texts such as the *Shurangama Sutra, Diamond Sutra, Lotus Sutra, Treatise on the Doctrine of Consciousness-Only, Nyayapravesha, Amitabha Sutra,* etc. On the side he also studied the teachings of Christianity and Confucianism. After age fifty he continued studying the *Lotus Sutra,* the vinayas, the *Lankavatara Sutra,* and the *Awakening of Mahayana Faith.* Among his works the one with the longest chapters was the

Entry into the Tripitaka, with forty-four chapters in total, and it was completed when he was fifty-six. In the same year, he also completed the five chapters of *Observing the Waves of the Dharma Sea*, and ten chapters of *The Ten Essences of Pure Land*, and he passed away in the following year.

Chapter 5 was a discussion on the formation and development of Master Ouyi's thought. Between ages twelve to thirty-three his thought took two directions: first, using the *Shurangama Sutra* as the center, he discussed the issues between the Chan and Pure Land schools; second, using Chan as the center, he discussed the issues of the *Vinaya*. In middle age his thoughts could be divided into the first and second stage. The first stage—between thirty-one to thirty-nine years old—he focused on the infusion of the thoughts of Dharma nature and the Dharma phenomena (Consciousness-Only), and he also used the *Brahma Net Sutra* as the center for his "essence of the mind" thought.

The second stage—between ages forty to forty nine—his thoughts were a reemphasis on the *Shurangama Sutra* and he proposed his theory of practice developed from the infusion and absorption of various schools. He associated the teaching and practice of the Tiantai school with the Consciousness-Only concepts, and at the same time, concluded with the Pure Land concepts. In his later years—between ages fifty to fifty seven—his thoughts emphasized the *Lankavatara Sutra* and the *Awakening of Mahayana Faith*, and he accomplished his purpose of delineating the theories on the harmonization between nature and phenomena, and the union of various schools. The reason was that the *Lankavatara Sutra* was counted as a sutra of the Tathagatagarbha system, but it also contained the Consciousness-Only thoughts of "the five characteristics of dharmas, the three aspects of nature, the eight consciousnesses, and the two kinds of selflessness." Therefore, it was a sutra that had the thoughts of the Dharma nature school of the Tathagatagarbha system, and it also had the thoughts of the Dharma Phenomena school of the Consciousness-Only system. the *Awakening of Mahayana Faith* also talked about the Dharma nature concepts of the Tathagatagarbha and True Suchness, and the thoughts of the Dharma Phenomena school of the alaya consciousness (fundamental consciousness). Master Ouyi stood at such a standpoint and viewed all the sutras as mutually harmonious, and he treated the sutras of both the nature and phenomena systems with equal weight.

I mentioned before that the scholars always recognized Master Ouyi as a Tiantai scholar. Actually, he only left four works related to the Tiantai school: (1) *Summary on the Meaning of Lotus Sutra*, sixteen chapters; (2) *Abstract of the Essential Meaning of Lotus Sutra*, two chapters; (3) *The Integrated Teaching of Lotus Sutra* (Chn. *Fahua Lunguan*), one chapter; (4) *Essential Guidelines for Teaching and Contemplation and Commentaries*, two chapters. However, according to himself, he wrote *Summary on the Meaning of Lotus Sutra* simply to illustrate and introduce the important concepts of the predecessors in simplified language as a convenience for those new to the practice, and he didn't add his own comments. *Essential Guidelines for Teaching and Contemplation* also had no new discussions, and he only organized the five periods (or divisions of Shakyamuni's teaching), the eight kinds of doctrines, the six identicals, and the ten vehicles of contemplation in detail.

He explained and introduced the four modes of conversion or enlightenment: direct (or sudden), gradual, esoteric, and variable; the four periods of teaching: Hinayana, interrelated, differentiated, and complete (or final); along with the ten vehicles of contemplation, and the six identicals. He grasped the essence of the Tiantai thinking on the dual emphasis on the teaching of theories and meditation practice, and allowed later generations to easily comprehend the complex Tiantai thoughts within a short period of time. He stood at the Tiantai standpoint, and of course one could say that he was expounding the Tiantai thoughts, and that he was a Tiantai scholar. However, he was not specialized in Tiantai only, and his purpose was to facilitate the grand aspect of the union of Buddhism. It could be said that in Master Ouyi's era, Buddhism in the late Ming Dynasty was under such a situation, and there was such a need for the harmonization between the nature and phenomena systems, between teaching and meditation practice, between Tiantai and Consciousness-Only schools, between Tiantai and Chan schools, and between Confucianism and Buddhism. The end result was to merge Chan, theoretical, vinaya, and esoteric teachings into the Western Pure Land of Amitabha.

After I completed this thesis, I discovered that Master Ouyi was very truthful and mindful in his life—on one hand he would fully engage himself in the practice of faith, and on the other hand he was working on expounding the Buddhadharma of the sutras, vinayas, and shastras, night and day, year after year. From the academic perspective he didn't belong to any school. Even in terms of the Western Pure Land, which he thought was his last refuge, he only left a *Commentary on the Amitabha Sutra* and a few single articles. His thoughts had lasting effects on Chinese Buddhism, even till after the Qing Dynasty and the early Republican Era. For example, it could be said that Master Ouyi influenced the contemporary Master Taixu's thought that "all eight schools are equal."

Among the three systems of Mahayana Buddhism in India,

Master Ouyi discussed the Dharma Nature school advocating True Suchness and Tathagatagarbha, and the Dharma Phenomena school of Yogachara (Consciousness-Only), but he left out the Madhyamaka of Nagarjuna and Aryadeva. The Consciousness-Only concepts he discussed were also not the orthodox Faxiang (Consciousness-Only) school's point of view. Nor did he refer to Master Ci'en Kueiji's (632-682) *Great Commentary on Consciousness-Only*, and instead used the Tiantai method and added a subject of "explanation of contemplating the mind." The "mind" referred to here was not the dominating mind of the eighth consciousness which the Consciousness-Only talked about, but the "original mind of all dharmas," so he used the concept of mind-only to explain Consciousness-Only. As a result, the title of his book [related to the consciousness thoughts] was *The Essence of Contemplating the Mind for the Treatise on the Doctrine of Consciousness-Only*. It was very clear that his intent was not on promoting the thought of Consciousness-Only.

Chapter 9

East and West

Completing the Doctoral Thesis

In January 1975, I submitted my doctoral thesis to the Office of the Doctorate School of Rissho University. It was accepted but I did not know whether it would be approved. The thesis was written with a fountain pen, stroke by stroke, neatly and orderly, word-by-word, on the standard size draft paper of 500 words per sheet, for a total of nearly 1,000 sheets. I bound them into three large books and photocopied many sets and handed them to each of the related professors of the thesis review committee. There were two methods for the thesis review: one, the Professor Committee would select suitable experts of 3 to 5 people to conduct a specialized review, and then all the professors of the Literature Department of the Doctorate School, the Eastern History Department, the Buddhist Department, and the Nichiren Sect Religious Department would conduct an oral exam. Second was an accountability policy—the chief and vice advisors would sign a recommendation to certify that the thesis had reached the doctoral degree standards, and then it would be reviewed and approved by all the members of the Professor Committee.

I was appointed to use the second method because in Japan the advisor must be fully responsible for the thesis he advised on. If a thesis was approved without reaching standards, it would be very unfavorable for the advisor. The professors all looked after their reputation and would not easily consent to approve a thesis.

Therefore, once the advisor certified and made a recommendation, the thesis could be counted as approved. Especially since my two previous and present chief advisors, Prof. Sakamoto Yukio and Prof. Kanakura Ensho, were both authoritative elders in Japanese academic circles. Prof. Kanakura was also a member of the Japan Academy, a person with national treasure status who was once president of the National Tohoku University. He specialized in the Philosophy of Indian Religions, but some of his works and translations were also related to Chinese Buddhism texts.

My co-advisor, Prof. Nomura Yosho, was an expert in Chinese Buddhist history, and had published ten or more works. The two professors had very high praise for my thesis. Prof. Nomura drafted the initial Review Report and after Prof. Kanakura read through it, he added some more emphatic words of praise. Even Prof. Nomura seemed quite surprised because Prof. Kanakura was known for his rigorous attitude in studies, and it was an honor to me that he would treat me this way.

The morning of February 12 of the same year, the atmosphere seemed a bit nervous at the whole Doctorate School. When my classmates and teachers saw me, they all seemed to be praying for me because there were twenty or more professors who would review my thesis, and even Prof. Kanakura and Prof. Nomura appeared to be nervous. The result of the review was that the chairman announced the approval by the whole committee. At the time the most joyful people didn't seem to be myself but my two advisors. They immediately stood up and thanked everyone and also congratulated me. The oral exam for this thesis was exceptionally smooth.

It wasn't painful to write the thesis but it took a lot of time and effort, and I also bothered many people. Every other week I would take the written draft to visit my two advisors in turn. I would read it to them face to face, and the draft was revised over and over again. It took up quite an amount of time for the two professors. Every time I visited their place, I would stay for half a day and this troubled the wives of the two professors to serve tea and desserts. Sometimes, they would order sushi from outside for my lunch and they also treated me dinner. After two years I almost became one of their family members, and had more chances to meet them than their own sons and daughters.

Besides, for the revision of the Japanese wording of my thesis, I also troubled many Japanese teachers and classmates, a total of seven of them. They were all good friends of mine, and among them Mr. Seiichi Kiriya helped me the most. Not only did he edit the entire thesis, he also helped me with the improvements on the organizational structure of the wordings. He accompanied me to the vacation center affiliated with the Nichiren sect at Hakone National Park and we enjoyed a three-day stay for half price, sharing a room. We didn't go there to see the scenery but to escape the noise of Tokyo. In those three days, besides eating, drinking, and sleeping, there was no telephone, no television and newspaper, and nothing to bother us; we just simply focused on proofreading my thesis. Consider that it was troublesome enough to read through a thesis of more than 400,000 words once; at the time we had to edit and correct it line by line. Where can one find such a good friend?

After one month and five days, which was the morning of March 17 of the same year, I was in the office of Prof. Sugaya Shokan, the President of Rissho University, who had invited me and my two advisors and several high level administrators as well as the secretary of the Doctorate School, for a tea party. Each of us had a piece of cake and a cup of coffee. After we finished the coffee and dessert, we had the diploma-issuing ceremony conferring the doctoral diploma. Afterwards, my title became Chang Sheng Yen, Litt. D. The president didn't say much, he only declared the content of the diploma and said, "Congratulations!" He handed me the diploma and after everyone clapped hands, the ceremony was completed. It seemed that being a Doctor of Literature wasn't all that glamorous; there was no grand ceremony, and no doctoral robes and caps to wear. If you went to any occasion or ceremony, nobody would know that you had the status of Doctor of Literature. I already knew about this; therefore, on that day I was well dressed in my monk's robes and sangha robes, and attended the ceremony as a bhikshu to express my gratitude towards the Three Jewels, and how I valued my bhikshu identity.

After the ceremony I saw in the president's office a portrait drawing of Nichiren Shonin, the founder of the Nichiren sect. I bowed deeply to his portrait three times to express my gratitude for completing this highest honor degree under the university established by his sect. In Japan at the time there was no degree such as Doctor of Philosophy, only Doctor of Literature. Anyone who did research in history, religion, literature, and philosophy would be conferred the Doctor of Literature. Among all the doctoral degrees, the most difficult to obtain was the Doctor of Literature. For the Japanese, they would always obtain the doctoral degree ten or twenty years after they completed the doctoral degree courses. In their view, the doctoral degree represented the summit of the scholar's study result. Only one who "reached the peak of perfection" could be conferred such an honor. It was very lucky for me to complete the doctoral degree courses, proposed my thesis, and received the academic degree within four years.

I Became an Overseas Scholar

After obtaining the doctoral degree, reasonably speaking, I had nothing more to do. However, my work was not completed and I had to publish my thesis in Japan. Therefore, I continued my stay in Tokyo. On one hand I tried to raise money for publishing expenses and on the other hand I contacted publishing companies. One could usually apply for subsidies for the publishing of similar academic theses from the Ministry of Education. Otherwise, no publishing company would dare to accept the project. There was not much of a market other than the specialists, scholars, and the schools' libraries that would acquire the degree theses. In April, I finally settled the matters with the owner of Tokyo Sankibo Busshorin, and agreed on publishing 500 copies, of which I had to buy half.

Its set price was 8,750 Japanese Yen per book, with 30% discount, and I ended up paying him 1,500,000 Japanese Yen. This money came from my savings over the years, and the help from Master Nanting in Taiwan, lay Buddhist Mr. C. T. Shen in America and his friend Shen Jiaying. There was no "house of treasure" in the books and all the reading and writing only resulted in a beggar because one had to beg for money to publish the books. During that time, I had to go to the publisher very often to look at the "baby to be born." The publishing standards of the Japanese publishers were quite high and they were very diligent. They proofread the thesis for a total of three times, and it was not an easy job to proofread that thesis because I used many Chinese characters in the book, and some of them were even old characters from the original texts that could not be altered. Therefore, it took a long time. After half a year the book was finally published, and that was November 23 of the same year.

During the stage of publishing my thesis, I was invited by our government to attend the Fourth National Development Convention for Overseas Scholars, "National Development Convention" for short. The reason for this was after I received the doctoral degree, I reported to our government's representative in Japan—Mr. Ma Shuli. Mr. Ma held a big celebration party at the Chinese restaurant Zuien in the Roppongi District of Tokyo on March 29. Soon afterwards, I received a joint invitation letter from the Ministry of Education, National Youth Commission, and the Youth Corps, inquiring whether I would be able to return to Taiwan to attend a convention. The result was that I became one of the 120 overseas scholars who were invited by the government to attend the meeting of the National Development Convention in 1975.

I always thought of myself as a monk; so how did I receive a doctorate in Buddhist literature in Japan, and a few days later in Taiwan, became an "overseas scholar"? My feelings at the time were that the Taiwanese government placed much emphasis on nurturing talents studying abroad. The ancient scholars had the motto: "scholars repay the country" and "return home with glory." For a monk like myself, personal prestige was trivial but there was a responsibility to the country and to Buddhism. Especially given that monks and nuns before me who studied Buddhism in Japan received the bachelor's and master's degrees, and entered the institutes to teach, yet were not recognized by the government. Now since the Ministry of Education, a government department, invited me to return to Taiwan to attend the convention, this should mean that the government accepted my credentials. Therefore, I was delighted to attend. On July 25 of that year, I returned to Taipei and showed up at the reception desk of the convention.

At this meeting I was able to contact many famous international overseas scholars, such as Mr. Lu Qiao, the author of *Son of Man* and of *Weiyang Ge*; Prof. Zhang Jinghu, who is the son of Mr. Zhang Qiyun; Prof. Luo Jintang of the University of Hawaii; Prof. Wu Xingyong of University of Washington in Seattle; Prof. Zhu Xianren of Florida University; Prof. Huang Kunyan of George Washington University; Prof. Qian Xi of Columbia University; Wu Yunxiang of the University of California; Zhang Heqin of Washington State University; Yang Jinghua of Tennessee University; Zhai Wenbo of New York City University; Liao Zhaoxiong of Boston University; Liu Dai of Delaware State University; Lu Jinlin of the National University in Spain, and other scholars of note. I had much conversation with them, as they were interested in Buddhism and Buddhist studies. Among them, some still stayed in contact with me after the meeting, and would give me a call every time they came to Taiwan.

At the meeting I also made contact with and got to know several high level government officials, such as the president of Taiwan at the time, Mr. Yan Jiagan; the Prime Minister Mr. Jiang Jingguo, the Minister of Education Mr. Jiang Yanshi, the director of the Youth Corps, Mr. Li Huan; the Chairman of the National Youth Commission, Mr. Pan Zhenqiu; the Executive Secretary of the National Youth Commission, Mr. Yao Shun; the Provincial Chairman Mr. Xie Dongmin, etc. The Vice Minister of Education Mr. Chen Lu'an even invited me to his house along with some of his good friends. We had an easy chat for the whole night, and focused on the issues of Buddhism and Buddhist studies.

I proposed three issues at the meeting, and the chairman of the convention, Dr. Gu Peimu appointed me to speak. This caused the camera of the TV stations to all focus on me. The three proposals were: (1) to bring religious education into the university system,

(2) to be aware of the reorganization of the "green light zones," i.e., brothels, and clear up underworld society of gangsters through social education, (3) to emphasize spiritual education, which means dual development of humanity and science.

Actually at this meeting, I contributed less yet gained a lot. A monk with the status of scholar studying abroad appearing on the domestic television and newspaper for several days consecutively caused the domestic people's impressions towards nuns and monks to be changed anew, and this was a major turning point for the image of Buddhism in Taiwan. However, the Buddhist community's reactions were of two extremes. Some lay Buddhists thought: there is a monk with a doctor's degree in the sangha who was a scholar studying abroad, so Buddhism "finally broke the ice." Another group would say, "A monk with a doctor's degree, what for? Who knows what he's up to? Everyone better watch out." Aside from Master Dongchu and a few elders and a few old lay Buddhists who were enthusiastic about my return to Taiwan, on average most people took the position of staying on cautious alert.

Actually at that stage there was not much I could do. It was exactly as one of my classmates from the Shanghai Buddhist Academy wrote to me, speaking metaphorically: "You may have learned how to drive from studying abroad and got the driver's license. Unfortunately, there is no car for you in our country. What can you do about it?" Although my Tonsure Master Dongchu hoped I could return to Taiwan to develop Buddhist education, it was easier said than done since I had no idea where to start. Therefore, soon after the meeting I returned to Tokyo. At the time, Mr. C. T. Shen invited me to come to the United States to teach, so under such causes and conditions, I left Tokyo on December 10 of the same year, and went to the United States.

Reality Caused Me to Change My Profession

Mr. C. T. Shen lived in the East Coast of the United States and was originally a tycoon in the shipping business. He had good relations with Mr. Dong Haoyun of Orient Steam Navigation Co., Ltd. As a result, that company transported a large bundle of my books from Tokyo to New York for free. However, the ships of Mr. Shen's company all traveled the domestic route. Since he believed in Buddhism, he supported Buddhism piously. When I was studying in Tokyo, the scholarship from Switzerland was probably his support, although even up to the present, he has not openly admitted this. However, I thought that other than Mr. Shen, there could be no other person. Prior to his support for me, he also once sponsored another monk, who returned to lay life, to study abroad in Japan. Unfortunately, that person did not complete his studies.

Mr. Shen handed me the invitation letter issued by the Buddhist Association of the United States, of which he was a founder. Originally, I was hoping to do several more years of studies in the Institute for World Religions at State University of New York at Stony Brook, which he established. However, according to Mr. Shen, he thought that a monk should live in the monastery, and there should be someone to expound on the Dharma for the Buddhist Association of the United States, so he arranged me to stay at the Temple of Enlightenment in the Bronx borough of New York City.

It was really ridiculous. Seven years ago I went to Japan without being able to understand Japanese; now I am in America without being able to understand English. Therefore, after I settled in New York, Mr. Shen sent me to language school to study for four hours a day, and five days a week. He arranged a one-on-one teacher, which cost 14 US dollars per hour. I studied for half a year consecutively and changed three schools, and then I studied inconsecutively for half a year more. I spent a lot of Mr. Shen's money, and just as Mr. Shen had said, "After forty years old, it's harder to learn another foreign language from the start." Although afterwards, my English teacher became my student in learning Chan, and would often be my English tutor for free, yet even till the present, I had not learned English well. I could read but very slowly, and I could listen, but sometimes I need the other person to say it again. I could speak but did not have much vocabulary, and I could write but I would have to ask someone to do corrections for me.

However, there were many reasons why I did not learn English well. In America, the monastic life, the monastic administrations, and the reception of followers did not allow me much time to review my English studies. In addition most of the members of the Buddhist Association of the United States were Chinese, and since I used Chinese with them, I did not have the chance to practice English. Especially after 1978, every three months, I had to return to Taiwan. After living in Taiwan for three months then returning to America, I had already forgotten the English I learned. When in America I gradually made progress in my English skills, but after going back to Taiwan again, I lost a lot of the skills. Another factor was that some of my American disciples could speak Chinese, and among my Chinese disciples, some had very good English talents. As a result, some American disciples would speak to me in Chinese, and my Chinese disciples would translate my Chinese into English, so there was no need for me to speak English.

I lived at the Temple of Enlightenment for less than two years. In order to contact and guide Westerners and spread the Dharma to the society of Westerners, it was not enough nor attractive to just speak with the mouth. The Americans emphasize practicality and efficiency, so the best way was to let them recite mantras or learn Chan and meditation. Up till the present time Tibetan Esoteric Buddhism and Japanese Zen were the mainstream for Westerners who contacted and were learning Buddhism. The Buddhism of Southeast Asia, which used the shamata-vipashyana method, was also popular in the West. Therefore, I also used the meditation method I learned in Mainland China and in the mountains in Taiwan, as well as the meditation format I observed in Japan, to teach Westerners the concepts and sitting methods of Chan. As a result, I transformed from a Doctor of Literature recently awarded and became a Chan Master teaching Chan. I never expected such a quick change in profession.

Chan Master, Scholar, and Educator

In December 1977, Master Dongchu passed away in Taiwan. After receiving an overseas phone call, I immediately returned to Taiwan to deal with his funeral arrangements. I followed his will and inherited the abbotship of his monastery and became the director of the Chung-Hwa Institute of Buddhist Culture. Afterwards, I traveled back and forth between America and Taiwan, and looked after both the East and the West.

I established the Chan Meditation Center in New York, and the original members were mainly Westerners with a few Chinese. I held regular meditation activities and Chan retreats consecutively for several times. For the purpose of teaching, I compiled a small book, *The Experience of Chan*. Its contents included the origin of Chan, the basic methods, changes in the style of Chan, the enlightenment and demonic states, etc. It was used to teach those who were learning Chan from me about the correct concepts and safe methods. It was my first book related to the study of Chan. My teachings in the Chan retreats and the regular lectures were gradually being organized into manuscripts, and two English publications were published regularly: *Chan Magazine*, a quarterly, and *Chan Newsletter*, a monthly. Up until the end of 1992, *Chan Magazine* has published up to Issue No.58, and *Chan Newsletter* to Issue No.96.

They were being widely distributed in 36 countries in America, Asia, Europe, Africa, and Australia. Therefore, our Chan Meditation Center in New York already became a well-known center on the world map of meditation centers. At the same time, from 1982 onwards, we established Dharma Drum Publications for publishing English Chan teachings. It published my English works, and up till the end of 1992, eight texts were published. The Element Publishing in London England also published a book of my retreat talks. What was unbelievable to me was that a publisher in Rome, Italy, Ubaldini Editore, Roma, translated my commentaries on *Faith in Mind* into Italian and published it in 1991. The title of the book was *Credere Nella Mente*.

For the past 16 years, since holding over 60 Chan retreats in English-speaking countries in Europe and America, the Buddhist community has recognized me as a Chan Master. As a result, many Western meditation groups invited me to instruct and introduce the teachings and methods of Chinese Chan to them. Up until the time I wrote this book, I was invited to forty or more universities in various countries in America and Europe and mainly in the United States, including Ivy League universities, to give over 100 lectures.

From 1978 onwards I also held Chan retreats in Taiwan for college students and the general public at the Chung-Hwa Institute of Buddhist Culture in Beitou, and at Nung Chan Monastery. In a blink of an eye 15 years had passed, and I have held over 44 Chan retreats in Taiwan. In this period I compiled, lectured, wrote, and completed seven Chan related works. Among them were two new compilations of ancient Chan materials: *The Essentials of Practice and Attainment within the Gates of Chan* (Chn. *Chanmen xiuzheng zhiyao*) and *The Dragon's Pearl: an Anthology of Chan Masters* (Chn. *Chanmen lizhuji*). *Chan and Daily Living* (Chn. *Chan de shenghuo*), *Holding a Flower with a Smile* (Chn. *Nianhua weixiao*), and *Chan and Enlightenment* (Chn. *Chan yu wu*) were my speech notes and thesis. These five books were well received domestically. In 1991, the Yuanshen publisher in Taipei entrusted the author, lay Buddhist Mr. Lin Qingxuan, to collect and compile them into three books titled *The Three Essentials of the Gates of Chan*. The book sold very well on the market and many people in Taiwan regarded me as a Chan Master as a result.

As mentioned in the first section of Chapter 3, I received Dharma transmission in both the Linji and Caodong lineages, and also had experiences of meditation practice. Prior to my arrival in America, I never considered becoming a Chan Master to teach meditation. Since the causes and conditions have led to such an arrangement, I followed through with the opportunity to spread the teaching of Chan. However, from my other achievements, one could not say that I was a Chan Master.

In 1978, the founder of Chinese Culture University, Professor Zhang Qiyun (1900-1985) hired me to take on the position of professor at their Institute of Philosophy, and president of the Institute of Buddhist Studies at their affiliated China Academy. This allowed me to enter the education arena and carry on the work of education and academic research in Taiwan. Although I still had to travel between the East and the West every three months, luckily,

Master Chengyi of the Taipei Huayan Lotus Society took up the responsibility of vice president, and professor Li Zhifu shared several administrative works. Besides teaching, I also had to attend to the Hwakang Buddhist Journal, which wasn't a heavy job. Due to this job, I had the opportunity to be in contact with the young students and benefited from learning and growing through the teaching job. Meanwhile, I kept in contact with the scholars doing research in Buddhist studies at the time and also had to write research papers myself.

In 1985 because the university was upgraded to Culture University, and there were changes in policy and personnel, I resigned from the duties at that university. Under the encouragement and expectations from several friends and students, I established the Chung-Hwa Institute of Buddhist Studies on the premises of Chung-Hwa Institute of Buddhist Culture in Beitou, and published the Chung-Hwa Buddhist Journal, a yearly. In July 1987, the Chung-Hwa Institute of Buddhist Studies was approved by the Ministry of Education as a B class institute, and we were approved to recruit postgraduate students at the master's degree course level, but we would not confer a degree. However, the qualifications of our teachers, facilities, applicants, and the number of students recruited all met the Ministry of Education's Standards for A class institutes. Within three years of a course program, the students would also have to take at least two language courses, and complete the full 36 course credits, plus a thesis in order to graduate. Therefore, the students would have the actual education level of the master's degree. Among the graduated students, many of them have been awarded the state scholarship and studied abroad in the national universities in Japan. There were a few monastic students who had completed their studies at Tokyo Imperial

University and obtained their doctoral degrees. They have returned to Taiwan to provide their services.

I taught at the Chinese Culture University and the later promoted Culture University, Soochow University, and the Chung-Hwa Institute of Buddhist Studies. The subjects that I taught included studies in Huayan, Tiantai, Pure Land, Madhyamaka, Yogachara and Chan. After I taught for several years, the students found their way to the door of understanding, and I ended up understanding more than the students. The saying "a rising tide lifts all boats" was an unchanging rule. I was very grateful for this kind of opportunity. For example, since I had to teach *Chapters on the Five Teachings of Huayan*, I read many Huayan related works, and since I had to teach Yogachara, I collected all the commentaries and theses I could find on the *Treatise on the Doctrine of Consciousness-Only*. Since I had to teach Madhyamaka, I read all the ancient and contemporary commentaries and research on *Madhyamaka Shastra* as well as all its different translated versions. All these subjects were left out in my course of studies when I was studying in the past.

At the time I had this attitude: if I didn't understand a lot or specialize in my studies, it didn't matter because I would request my students to outdo the teacher after listening to the classes. If I wasn't that good, that's fine, but I would honestly tell my students that they should not use me as their standard. They should use what level they could perform to as their standard. This was also very useful. For example, my student Master Huimin, who listened to my Madhyamaka and Yogachara classes, completed his studies at the Tokyo University in Japan and obtained his doctoral degree. He returned to Taiwan and replaced me in teaching these two courses, and he was teaching better than I did. Professor Cheng Yingshan, who audited my Huayan and Tiantai classes, was currently teaching these two courses at our institute.

Gradually, I handed over the Chan studies and Pure Land studies to the younger generation, such as Master Huiyan, who held a Doctor of Literature from Bukkyo University in Japan. I was a pioneer opening up a small trail in virgin land, trying to modernize Buddhist education, but for a broader path, that would have to rely on the continuous efforts of the young talents in the future.

I never received a modern university education and I didn't even study high school. Therefore, it would seem that I was not the most suitable candidate to develop education, nor a very good teacher. However, there was a local idiom in Hokkien that said, "When there is no ox then use the horse." Therefore, when there was no ox, a skinny horse like me could be used as a substitute. However, it was a fact that I was undertaking the educational work at the research institutes.

Furthermore, I was one of the founding members of the International Association of Buddhist Studies, which would take turns in holding a Theses Presentation Conference in various countries of the world every two years, and I was invited to attend each time. At the same time, our Institute of Buddhist Studies published the *Chung-Hwa* Buddhist Journal, issued yearly. Every issue would contain 200,000 to 400,000 words, and I had to write a thesis of academic research every year. Some of them were continuous research on the late Ming Buddhism. In other words, those were the continuing work on my doctoral thesis, and each of them was written in Chinese and then translated into English.

In 1987, I combined four of these theses into a book *Studies in Late Ming Dynasty Buddhism* (Chn. *Mingmo fojiao yanjiu*), with a total of 200,000 words. The theses were: (1) *The Chan Figures and Their Characteristics in the Late Ming Dynasty*, (2) *The Pure Land Figures and Their Thoughts in the Late Ming Dynasty*, (3) *The Conscious Only Scholars and Their Thoughts in the Late Ming Dynasty*, (4) *The Buddhism of Lay Buddhists in the Late Ming Dynasty*. Due to the book title, many people mistook it to be the Chinese translation of my doctoral thesis. Actually, my doctoral thesis was translated by Mr. Guan Shiqian and forwarded to the Student Book Co., Ltd in Taipei for publishing in 1988, and it was categorized as their fifth religious book series.

Although not many people read my doctoral thesis and its further work, they already became one of the texts collected by the larger public and private libraries worldwide under their Asian section. Any scholar doing research on the issues of the Ming and Qing dynasties would refer to these two books. As a result, although not many people read them they still had their use. Therefore, I was undoubtedly a scholar recognized internationally.

Chapter 10

Traveling and Writing

Footprints in the Snow

When I was young I had the habit of writing in diaries. I read several diaries written by others and not only could I see the author's life, but also their thoughts, emotions, and character. Through the author's capacity to convey their observations and experiences with words, the reader could enter the author's spiritual world and share their feelings and interests in life. Through reading such diaries one could gain knowledge and inspire one's wisdom, and by following through the tone of the pen, one could journey along with the author, return to the past, work in the present, and hope for the future. A diary like this would be a presentation of life, with blood and flesh, joy and pain, tears as well as laughter. However, such a work was rare to see.

Who am I? I had no literary background and not many thoughts, definitely unlike many writers on literature and art who were full of overflowing emotions. Therefore, I couldn't write very good diaries. However, when I began studying abroad in Japan, I wrote in my diary every day, just a few simple lines about my everyday life, much simpler than the memoir type of diary. Since I didn't plan on writing a memoir, the diaries were of not much use to me and I didn't pay much attention to them. After several moves and relocations, most of them were lost and gone.

However, I still kept and continued my habit of writing diaries. I described such diaries as "footprints in the snow." When I was writing them, they appeared to be vivid and profound because they were part of the process of my life and experience. However, after some time, they often appeared to be unimportant anymore. It was like someone walking in the snow, with one step, one footprint, very clear and vivid. After one walked past, the falling snow would soon cover their footprints, and when the snow melted away, the footprints would be gone too.

However, if I thought that my "footprints" would temporarily benefit others, I would do my best to write them into articles and reported them to others. For example, when I was studying in Japan, I wrote 20 or more such articles. After I went to the United States, if I participated in public events and first-time visits, I would mostly write them up as articles and reported them through publications in Taiwan. Such similar works, I also referred to them as footprints in the snow. Perhaps not many people would notice footprints in the wilderness in snowy weather. However, one who marched in the wilderness in a heavy snowstorm surely was not anticipating others to notice their footprints in the snow, but to know for themselves that one must continue in the snow for the purpose in mind.

When I wrote articles or travel journals, I mostly used my simple daily diaries as basis. My motivation was simply to share with others what I know. Actually, after writing them I was the one who benefited the most. If I didn't write down the events I experienced, the people I met, the books I read, and the environment I was in, then these events wouldn't leave any lasting impression, and they wouldn't become real experiences. Therefore, as long as time permitted and it was worth writing about, I would write them up as articles afterwards. I would even compile them into books, as reference for myself and to report them to the readers. Since 1988 up to the present (1992), I have published five books of travel journals written in prose.

The Homeland: Separated for Thirty-Nine Years

In the spring of 1988, I returned to my birthplace in Mainland China after thirty-nine years away. At that time, I was not prepared to write any articles on this. However, after returning to New York after the 19-day visit, the process during that period was so vivid that I couldn't erase them from my mind. Therefore, I took up the pen to write. Originally, I only wanted to write a few thousand words to express the feeling that was caught in my mind. Unexpectedly, after I started writing, I couldn't stop, and within a few days, I wrote a whole lot to complete a book. In October of the same year, I handed them to our Dongchu Press for publishing, and the book was titled *Spring of Dharma, Source of Life*.

The book began with my receiving a letter from my nephew from home, and I wrote about my journey back to my hometown. I went from Taiwan to Hong Kong to Beijing, and then traveled to the Great Wall, Dingling Tomb, Fayuan Monastery in Beijing, Buddha Tooth Relic Pagoda, and Yonghegong (the Lama Temple). I then traveled to Luoyang, visited the Longmen Grottoes, White Horse Temple, Shaolin Temple, and then went to Xian, and visited Xingjiao Monastery, Da Xingshan Monastery, Da Ci'en Monastery, Dayan (Big Wild Goose) Pagoda and Xiaoyan (Small Wild Goose) Pagoda.

I then flew from Xian to Shanghai, and saw my relatives from home: three elder brothers, one elder sister's husband, and groups of the sons and daughters as well as grandsons and granddaughters of my siblings. At the same time, I visited the Jing'an Monastery, which I once studied at, the Jade Buddha Temple, and the Longhua Monastery. I then boarded the Changjiang Ferry, and traveled to Wolf

Mountain in Nantong to visit the monastery where I first became a monk.

I also visited my elder sister's grave, which was nearby. Then I returned to the old home of my youth, the Changyinsha at the Southern bank of Yangzi River. I lit incense, candles, and recited sutras, said prayers in front of the graves of my parents and grand parents. Lastly, I visited Jiangtian Monastery in Jinshan Mountain at Zhenjiang as well as Jiaoshan Dinghui Monastery, where my deceased master, Master Dongchu, received Dharma transmission.

Being an old monk nearly in my sixties, I constantly felt sentimental throughout my visit. I shed many tears, some flowing inward, some flowing outward, and sometimes I cried without tears. The places I visited were the wellspring and development of Dharma in our country and also the source of life of my home relatives. Buddhism came to China from India, and after two thousand years of passing on the Dharma, it was indeed profound and long-lasting.

This time I went to the White Horse Temple in Mainland China, which was a Buddhist monument from the Han Dynasty. The story of the white horse carrying the sutras happened at the time of Emperor Mingdi of the Han Dynasty. The history of the Shaolin Temple happened at the time of the Emperor Wudi of the Liang Dynasty (502-557), when Bodhidharma faced the wall in meditation for nine years. It was a popular folklore in China. Xingjiao Monastery was the burial place of Master Xuanzang of the Tang Dynasty. Da Xingshan Monastery was built in the period of Emperor Xuanzong of Tang Dynasty. It was the home base for the so called Three Great Masters of the Kaiyuan Period who transmitted the esoteric Buddhism from India: Masters Shan Wuwei (Subhakarasimha), Vajra-bodhi, and Bukong (Amoghavajra). Da Ci'en Monastery was the location of the translation institute where Master Xuanzang translated the Buddhist sutras.

However, at the time I visited, I only saw a few old monks tending the gardens and they were there to serve the visiting tourists. These old monks were forced to return to lay life during the Cultural Revolution and before then. After 1980, they were gradually called back to the monasteries. They lived a very harsh life, and they had no freedom to teach the Dharma. Although some of them had become a monk in their youth, very few of them were able to receive the appropriate education. Of course, in present day Mainland China one can no longer see the aspects of Buddhism of Han (206 BCE-220 CE), Wei (220-265), Western Jin (265-316) and Eastern Jin (317-420) dynasties, Southern and Northern dynasties (420-589), and the prime time of the Tang Dynasty (618-907). Even the folk belief of mixed Buddhism and faith in deities was also uncommon.

Every place I went, I discovered that the monasteries were divided into two parts: the gardens for visiting tourists, and the area for devotees to burn incense and prostrate to the buddhas. Actually, according to their own admission, among the crowds who visited the monasteries, only one-tenth were devotees who came to burn incense and to prostrate to the buddhas.

As for my blood relatives, although we appeared to be well acquainted at the time we met—especially the few elder brothers who were all full of tears and sniffling—but after being separated for all these years, their lives, concepts, and values were all completely different from mine. I could understand their feelings in their hearts, but they could not understand what I was thinking, doing, and saying. They could only accept some of the material support from me, but they could not agree with my support for them on the level of faith.

During my stay with several older brothers, I was only able to talk my second brother into reading the sutras and reciting the names of the buddhas. Their impression was that I was still their younger brother before I became a monk. In fact, I was not that person anymore. Although they had suffered many vicissitudes and gone through life and death several times, it was a shame that they did not have that kind of feelings and understanding.

Of course, when I went with them to make offerings at our parents' graves, the atmosphere was solemn and focused. Everyone listened to me as I recited the sutras and the names of the buddhas. The three generations of the old and the young totaled 40-50 people, and they all listened in silence. After they saw me finish reciting the sutra and silently shedding tears in front of the grave, they also accompanied me in weeping. This made me feel that my blood relatives were indeed my relatives.

Therefore, at the very end when they accompanied me to the Shanghai airport, and as I was about to depart, I had a feeling of separation between life and death, and that they were sending me across the line of the living and the dead. One nephew, the eldest son of my third brother, after accompanying me for several days, changed the way he addressed me from the initial "uncle" to "Master Sheng Yen." This made me feel that the trip was worthwhile.

As a result, when I wrote towards the end of my travel journal, "Instead of this trip of visiting my relatives in Mainland China being a 'returning to the roots' I could say that I returned to the springtime of my life and the source of the Dharma, and that I also made a pilgrimage in search for the roots." If my blood relatives and I were all like birds, then I could fly and they couldn't. I wouldn't say that they were a group of birds in a cage because I was not a bird outside the cage myself. No matter how high I fly, I could not fly away from this earthly world.

After the book was published, it received popular acceptance because it was full of feeling and knowledge. It should be a travel journal with a harmony of knowledge and sensibility. After the second year, in 1989, it was recommended to be one of the candidates for the Jiaxin Literature Award for prose literature. Although I did not receive an award, but to be listed as a candidate meant that the book had received attention from the literary community.

My Journey to the West

When I was in my youth, I read Wu Cheng'en's *Journey to the West*, and knew that Master Xuanzang of Tang, on his journey to the west to retrieve the sutras, had to go through eighty-one obstacles. Although his Dharma protector, his Monkey King disciple Qitian Dasheng (the great saint who could match the heavenly beings), had the ability to change into 72 forms, and accompanied him on his journey, but still many disasters happened. At the time, I sympathized with Master Xuanzang who encountered obstacles one after another, yet enjoyed reading the exciting stories of Sun Wukong (the Monkey King disciple) charging to the rescue. After I read through the eighty-one obstacles, I was hoping for a further obstacle to continue reading on.

When I was older, I read the *Great Tang Records on the Western Regions*, written by Master Xuanzang, and I found it not as splendid as *Journey to the West*. However, the customs, culture, religion, and geographical locations he recorded on the Western Regions, especially concerning the distribution of the Buddhist sangha and their Dharma teaching and learning activities at the time made a deep impression on me. Although the transliterated names of people, objects, and locations sounded very unfamiliar to me, with patience, I still finished reading the book.

In the autumn of 1989, I went on a trip to India by myself, which was the Western Regions where Master Xuanzang traveled to during the Tang Dynasty. However, when Master Xuanzang traveled to the various countries in the west, he endured many difficulties and hardships on the way, and it took him 14 years. My trip was either on the plane, or on the bus, and it only took me 15 days. Therefore, it was not comparable to Master Xuanzang's journey to the west in any aspect.

My purpose for going to India was simply for the pilgrimage because in the beginning of that year, our Chung-Hwa Institute of Buddhist Studies began a greater project: we bought an area of land on the slope of the mountains at Jinshan Township, Taipei County, and we prepared to develop it into a world Buddhist education center, with multiple purposes such as education, culture, and practice, etc. Therefore, we established the Association of Dharma Supporters to develop fund-raising for its construction, and to use the collective efforts and strategic planning of the group to promote the concept of constructing such a monastery.

Buddhism originated in India, and for Buddhism today and Buddhism tomorrow, we should shed the tone of superstition, inactivity and escapism, and restore the wisdom and compassion of the enlightened Shakyamuni Buddha. We should return to the original intention of the Buddha and put our efforts into purifying the troubled human world. Therefore, I organized and formed the India and Nepal Pilgrimage Group of a core of eighty monastic and lay members to pay homage to the historic remains from the era of

Shakyamuni Buddha. The purpose was to encourage and inspire our group members to have the mind of seeking the Dharma, practicing the Dharma, upholding the Dharma, and spreading the Dharma.

After the pilgrimage trip and having returned to America, I thought about the spiritual comforts, inspiring knowledge, and encouragement of faith the *Great Tang Records on the Western Regions* and *Journey to the West* had given me. I told myself, "Although this journey only lasted for 15 days, I should still write it down for myself and the whole group members to renew our faith and retain our memories. As a result, I wrote and published the book titled *Pilgrimage to the Land of the Buddha* (Chn. *Foguo zhilu*).

The Nepal of today was once part of the Western Regions, and the birthplace of Shakyamuni Buddha was within the region of Nepal. It was located between the two regions of Tibet and India. A part of Tibetan Buddhism came from India through Nepal, and part of the current Tibetan Buddhism grew within the regions of Nepal. Our visit to India also took the route from Nepal to India because it was more convenient. Therefore, the first stop of our journey was Kathmandu, the capital of Nepal.

We stayed there for three days, and visited the local Buddhist monuments and the lamaseries of Tibetan tradition. We then flew out from Nepal valley and arrived at the remains of the Nalanda monastery, where Master Xuanzang studied, taught, and held the debate conventions. We then visited the famous city at the time of the Buddha Rajagriha and the nearby Veluvana. Next we visited the sacred site, Gridhrakuta (Vulture) Mountain, where Shakyamuni Buddha expounded the *Lotus Sutra*, and then we visited Bodhgaya, the place where Shakyamuni Buddha reached enlightenment, and the stupa (great tower) and the bodhi tree there. We visited Varanasi and the nearby Kushinagar (Buddha's place of nirvana) and the monuments of cremation. At the same time, we also enjoyed the precious beautiful sunrise scenery at the bank of the Ganges River.

We then visited the monuments and museum at Sarnath, the place where, after his enlightenment, the Buddha first turned the wheel of the Dharma to deliver his five bhikkhu (Pali for "bhiksu") followers. We then returned to Nepal, and visited the Buddha's birthplace Lumbini, and from Nepal entered India and visited another famous monastery at the time of the Buddha—Jeta Grove Monastery of Anathapindada's Garden. The pilgrimage ended, and to board the direct flight to Hong Kong and America, we arrived at New Delhi where the current Indian government was located, and we visited the famous architectural sites and ancient castles in the surrounding areas, which were the remains from the era of several Muslim Kingdoms.

In this journey, I felt grateful, sentimental and aspiring. The Dharma was able to be passed down due to the birth of the Buddha, which allowed countless sentient beings over the years to receive spiritual comfort, and have refuge in life and faith. How could we not feel grateful? Therefore, at the place where the Buddha attained enlightenment, near the Bodhgaya Stupa, there was a stela (stone pillar) in memoriam for the Mahabrahma-deva's (The King of the Heavens) request for the Buddha to expound the Dharma. After I prostrated at the sight, I felt so grateful that I could hardly stand up. I witnessed that the places, Veluvana, Jeta Grove, Gridhrakuta, and Sarnath, where the Buddha taught the Dharma and delivered sentient beings, were all in wilderness and not even torn-down walls or broken ruins could be seen. There were only a few red bricks covered on the floor to symbolize the footings of the bases of the original structures, and there was virtually nothing left.

At the same time, surrounding New Delhi, one could see construction materials of monasteries left over from the several Muslim Kingdoms. I've heard that they were torn down from ten or more Buddhist monasteries. How could one not feel sorrow and desolation in the mind after seeing stone Buddhist statues that had their nose chopped away, eyes plucked out, ears cut off, and hands torn off? It was because the Buddhists lacked talents, and the invasion of the Muslims from the north, resulted in the end of Buddhism in India after the 14th and 15th centuries, and it was a complete extinction.

However, after the end of the Second World War in 1945, Jawaharlal Nehru assumed the position of the Prime Minister of India. Although he was a Hindu follower, he instructed the government to set specific funding for rediscovery and reorganization of the various Buddhist monuments within India, and set up museums for Buddhist historical monuments. This allowed the Buddhists worldwide to be in a trend of traveling to India for pilgrimage of the Buddhist sacred monuments. Especially Buddhists in Japan, Sri Lanka, Myanmar (Burma), Thailand, and Tibet would pilgrimage in groups to India to visit the eight great holy sites of Buddhism.

The Chinese already established monasteries at the eight great holy sites. Although very few people from Mainland China would go on pilgrimage, there were many Chinese from Taiwan and Southeast Asia who went for pilgrimage. Buddhist activities gradually revived within India, and it was a fact that they had Buddhists in the country. As a result, I thought this called for the establishment of the common ethos for world Buddhists to restore the original features and aspects of Buddhism at the time of the Buddha, and that this was worth aspiring to.

Buddhism, after surviving for 2500 years, was like an old vine which though it had its old roots cleared away, its branches and shoots were still growing, and since the individual branches were separated, they seemed like strangers who didn't recognize one another. Fortunately, there was still a common source of the Dharma—the Buddha's monuments in India, which allowed the Buddhists of each individual branch to trace their source and search for their roots. This also gave world Buddhists a common ethos: to return to the original intention of the Buddha, and then unify each other's vision, harmonize the footsteps of development, and march on towards an integrated Buddhism of tomorrow. This was also the common wish of the visionaries in the world Buddhist community today.

On our pilgrimage, every time we arrived at a place, I would explain and introduce to our group members on the trip—before hand, on the spot, or afterwards—about the events concerning the Buddha that happened at that place, what the Buddha said, and what kind of inspiration we could get from it. Being there personally on the scene was much more realistic than giving lectures and teaching sutras in the classrooms in Taiwan. The scenes we saw and the roads we walked on were probably all described in the Buddhist sutras, and were probably the living environment where the Buddha and his arhat disciples had lived and walked on. As we walked in these places, we were also following the Buddha's footsteps, and walking towards the path of becoming a buddha and a bodhisasttva.

Therefore, almost every place we went, many people were moved to tears. The place where the Buddha gained enlightenment, Bodhgaya, was a distance of several hundred kilometers away from Sarnath, where he first turned the Dharma wheel to deliver the five bhikkhus. The Buddha walked all the distance on foot just to deliver these five people. Then as he was about to enter nirvana after forty-nine years of spreading the Dharma and delivering sentient beings by traveling to various countries, the Buddha walked all the way from Mahavana Vihara of Vaishali in the south, to Kushinagar in the north. The Buddha taught as he walked; every time he passed by a village, he would stop for a rest, and he would use the time of resting to speak the Dharma to the villagers along the way. When he arrived at the Sala Forest, he was already very exhausted, but he continued to speak the Dharma.

Before the Buddha entered nirvana, there was an old Brahmin named Subhadra, a 120-year-old wise ascetic, who had the five super-mundane powers, who came to request teachings from the Buddha. Upon hearing the words from the Buddha, he immediately became an enlightened arhat and became the Buddha's last disciple. At this point, the Buddha closed his eyes and entered into nirvana, and his mortal body left our human world. After listening to my explanations at each place, the members of our pilgrimage group would weep silently.

This pilgrimage trip to India was more useful than the two years of lectures I gave in Taiwan, and it allowed everyone to affirm their faith in establishing the Dharma Drum Mountain. Afterwards, we came up with the following four-fold common ethos: (1) Our vision: to improve human character and build a pure land on earth; (2) our spirit: to devote ourselves and benefit people in society; (3) our direction: to return to the original intention of the Buddha, and work for the purification of the world; (4) our approach: to promote comprehensive education and extend loving care to all.

I Was a Miner

From the Buddhist perspective, everyone had his or her own treasure.

Everyone had the wisdom and merit equivalent to that of the buddhas with nothing lacking. The only difference is that those who had discovered their treasures were called buddhas, and those who were yet to discover their treasures were called sentient beings. Therefore, the *Ratnagotravibhaga Shastra* used the analogy of "true gold in the mine" and "buried treasure" to encourage us that we should not demean ourselves, be in self-despair or give up easily, but we should work relentlessly to develop the original hidden treasures within us.

The *Lotus Sutra* described the Buddha teaching the Dharma as "expounding the Dharma," which meant helping sentient beings to be free from the web of ignorance and vexations, and to disclose the original treasures within every sentient being. It was also known as "disclosing the knowledge of the Buddha" and "displaying the wisdom of the Buddha." One with true wisdom must have true merit, because merit and wisdom were like two sides of a same coin, and they complement each other. Everyone had inherent wisdom, but still one had to rely on the teachings of Buddhadharma and use the Dharma discourses to disclose the treasures of wisdom and merit within sentient beings. Buddhadharma was like the tool for mining the treasures, and a Dharma teacher would be the miner who uses this tool.

I didn't have any invention myself; I just nurtured a little bodhi-mind from the Dharma. Therefore, I vowed to help any sentient being that needed help. I was only a miner using the tools of the Dharma to discover my own treasure and at the same time assist others in discovering their own treasures.

There was a saying: "the jade cannot be made into a vase without being cut and polished" and "an uncut gem does not sparkle." If one did not have any specialized knowledge, one could not even distinguish gem or jade stones from ordinary rocks, so how could one make them shine and sparkle? In Buddhism, sentient beings needed to be "delivered" or transformed, and in common vocabulary of society, everyone needed to be "educated." Our common ethos had two sayings: "to promote comprehensive education and extend loving care to all." Our education should begin with the parents' prenatal education during pregnancy. After the baby was born, from the infant stage, to childhood, youth, young adolescence, there were family education, school education, adult education, and old-age education for these various stages. For the different stages and in between the stages, there should be something to connect them all, and the thing that could accomplish such a mission of guidance and connection would be religious education.

Based on such a vision we established the Dharma Drum Buddhist Education Center. Although it was located on the mountain slope of Jinshan Township along the northern coast of Taipei County, Taiwan Province, the area of its outreach would be endless and countless humanity as a whole. Since everyone had his or her own treasure, those who promoted the common ethos of Dharma Drum Mountain were all miners and owners of the mine. We would help each other, working cooperatively with a common purpose in mind to discover the treasures of the mind, and to nourish the source of abundant blessings.

As a result, after I found the piece of land in April 1989 and until December 1990, I completed a travel journal titled *A Mine in Golden Mountain* (Chn. *Jinshan youkuang*), and it had a chapter titled *Searching for Treasure in the Mine*. The religious, cultural, educational, and social activities that I engaged in were for those having affinity with me, for them to mine and polish their own treasures of gold and jade and share them with people in society.

To fulfill my purpose of constructing Dharma Drum Mountain, whether in terms of the hardware for material infrastructure or software for resource development, I sought references from various aspects, and put in a lot of mind and effort in finding references for constructing the buildings. In the spring of 1991, I invited the important supervisors and specialists related to the construction of Dharma Drum Mountain, a total of 13 people including myself, to take a 20-day-visit to three provinces in Mainland China: Hebei, Shanxi, and Gansu. We investigated the architectural styles of ancient Chinese monasteries of the Tang, Song, Liao, Jin, and up to the Ming and Qing dynasties.

We visited the Tanzhe Monastery, the Jietan Monastery, the Yihe Garden, and the Imperial Palace in Beijing; the Fangshan Library for Stone Sutras and the Chongshan Monastery in Taiyuan. We studied the Tang style of Nanchan Monastery, the Liao style of Foguang Monastery, and the various Ming and Qing styles of monasteries in Wutai Mountain. We then went to Datong and visited the Yungang Grottoes, and the Liao Dynasty ancient structures of Shanhua Monastery and Huayan Monastery. We then flew to the Dunhuang Grottoes in Gansu, and visited the paintings and carving skills of the Thousand Buddhas Caves of the Magao Grottoes. We also visited the Maiji Mountain Grottoes, which was also in the Gansu Province, and studied the paintings and architecture of the grottoes from the period of the Northern Wei Dynasty.

We also visited one of the two major Tibetan Buddhist monasteries in China, Labrang Monastery in southern Gansu. When we arrived at Beijing, we specially visited the Fragrant Hill Hotel designed by the world famous architect I. M. Pei. On this journey,

I was much inspired, so after I finished my visit and left Mainland China in December of that year, I completed another travel journal titled *Cool Wind in the House of Fire*, and its subtitle was *The Trip of Chinese Buddhist Arts*. The reason being, on this field trip, besides the architectural arts there were also various Buddhist arts such as paintings, music, carvings, stone sutras, etc.

The ancient Chinese Buddhist arts that were retained more completely would be those in the north and northwest regions. Due to the natural dry weather climate, and the inconvenience of transportation on land, it was so fortunate that they were well preserved.

After giving thought and investigation, my visions regarding the architecture of Dharma Drum Mountain was mentioned in Chapter 15 of *Cool Wind in the House of Fire* (Chn. *Huozhai qingliang*), and it had three points:

(1) It should have the point of view of modern people, while looking back at the good traditions of historical culture, and hoping to lead the movement of innovation for the future culture. This was essentially what the Chinese proposed as "carrying on the past and opening up a new way for future" or "inheriting the past and inspiring the future." One could not forget the past nor could one not think for the future, yet the present is the present.

(2) The construction site should retain the original landscape, we could not move the hills to fill the valley, and we should preserve the native resources such as: rivers, springs, and the native growth of flowers, trees and plants.

(3) Within the scope of basic safety facilities, beauty, and practicality, we should do our best in adopting modern technology and construction materials, and the image and color tone should be localized.

We reached common grounds with our architect designer Mr. Chen Bosen: the appearance of the architecture on Dharma Drum Mountain should give people the feeling that it was a native growth sprouting from the ground rather than something stiffly forced onto the slope of the mountains. The tone of color should match with the local environment and complement one another. When people lived in these facilities, they should feel as if they were in a natural environment. Of course, currently we were still in the planning stage, and we were not sure what it would be like in the future, but hopefully our ideas could come true.

After I initiated the activity of the construction of Dharma Drum Mountain, my activities with the outside world became even more frequent. There were actively and passively established relations from domestic to international, from the East to the West. More and more relationships were established, and each of these relationships required our time and effort. Buddhism proposed "establishing affinities" and the secular world talked about "mutual benefit." As others participated in our activities, we should also care for others. As others supported us, we should also take care of them in return. If it was only a one-way need and supply, then the relationship would not last, and it would be against the spirit of Buddhism.

Therefore, after I visited Mainland China, in May 1991, I began another long journey. In the East, I went to Hong Kong and Taiwan, and in the West, I went to Hawaii, Colorado, Kansas, New Jersey, Florida, Louisiana, Texas, and Georgia States. Around the same time, I also went to Canada in Northern America, Costa Rica in the Middle-South America, and the furthest trip was to London and Wales in England. After a year, in October 1992, I completed another travel journal titled *The Four Directions* (*East West South North*, Chn. *Dongxi nanbei*).

Between April 4 and 10 of 1992, I did an architecture research trip to Japan, visiting the Buddhist monasteries, university dormitories and its related hardware design and facilities. I visited Tokyo and Kyoto in Japan for a week. In mid October, I went to the Czech Republic and Belgium and visited two universities there. In late October, I took ten days to visit nine universities in seven states in the Midwest and Eastern United States, giving 14 lectures. It seemed like I could finish another travel journal by the end of the year [published as *The Four Seasons* (Chn. *Chunxia qiudong*) in 1999].

It was not my original profession to write travel journals, but to preserve the records of my tracks, to learn from the experience of the ancients, and to absorb the wisdom of others, accomplishing the present, looking out for the future, to account for my own responsibility, and provide the relevant information to the readers, I wrote in my journals untiringly.

Chapter 11

Standing at the Crossroads
Looking at the Street Scenes

A Goal with No Goal

In my youth, classmates asked me what kind of monk I would be in the future. At the time I felt lost and simply replied: "I just want to be a monk!" When I became a monk for the second time at thirty, an older lay Buddhist (upasaka) heard that I was going for solitary retreat in the mountains to study the sutras, so he especially came to see me. When he saw me he asked: "A young and promising monk like you has a great future and boundless prospects; you must be the outstanding talent of Buddhism for tomorrow. There were four great masters in contemporary Chinese Buddhism: Master Yinguang, Master Hongyi, Master Xuyun, and Master Taixu. Whom would you emulate, and which path would you take?"

I could not agree with what he said and answered: "I could not possibly emulate Master Yinguang's Pure Land, Master Hongyi's precepts, Master Xuyun's Chan, and Master Taixu's teachings on the Dharma. According to my endowments and conditions, I couldn't be like any one of them." The upasaka Buddhist sighed and left. Actually, I really wanted to tell him that I would take a fifth path; that I would do what I can to learn the teachings of Shakyamuni Buddha, to learn as much as I can, to know as much as I can, and to put into action as much as I can. I would do my best but I would not dare compare myself to any of the ancients.

I remembered two mottos from my parents when I was young: One time, my father and I walked by a river where there was a flock of ducks. We scared them as we passed by, so they all jumped into the river and swam to the other shore. My father said, "Son, did you see how those ducks were swimming in the river? The bigger ducks swam a wider path, and the smaller ducks swam a narrower path. No matter— big ducks, little ducks, wide paths, narrow paths, they all swam across the river. If one did not swim, there would be no path, and one could not get across the river." My father said again: "Son! People are like that too. No matter—big talent, small talent, high status, low status, as long as one did his best, there would always be a path for him. Do not envy others, and do not look down on yourself."

Another time, my mother was doing house chores and several neighboring women came along and saw me on the side of the house, and they started to chitchat about me. One woman said, "This little boy was so nice, so smart! In the future, he could become a top person, and live in the penthouse of a top building." Another woman said: "Well, if he was lucky, he would live on the top floor of a top building. If he was not so fortunate, he would have to carry bricks." My mother took a glance at me and thanked them, she then said, "It doesn't matter if he lived on the top floor or carried bricks, as long as he doesn't become a thief." My parents were illiterates, very common people, but within the depth of their minds, they could utter such words of wisdom, which had a very profound influence on my life.

Since an early age my physique has been weak and prone to illness, so I didn't have too much desire. I didn't want to establish a title or status, and I didn't have a specific goal to be completed. I only walked along with causes and conditions, with steady footsteps, moving forward with diligent effort. Especially since I understood the Buddhadharma and received its benefits, I did not have my own endeavors or my own goals to reach; I only thought about how to learn and spread the Dharma. Instead of saying that the purpose of my effort was for my own future, one could say that they were done for promoting the Buddhadharma and facilitating its function in delivering the world.

Glancing back at the 60 and more years of my life, none of this was what I had planned or thought for beforehand. Since I had not planned anything in advance, I was able to achieve success one way or another and have been content with what came along the way. Since I did not have a specific goal to achieve or the idea of something that must be accomplished, I felt at ease and I didn't put too much pressure on myself, so I wouldn't be influenced by the environment or heavy pressure from others. If it was something that I should do and I could do, of course I would do it. If it was something that should be done, but I couldn't do, then I wouldn't do it. I was still mortal, and it's impossible for me to not be moved at all by gains and losses, fame and fortune. However, through my understanding of the Buddhadharma, I learned that these problems could be quickly dissolved through self-adjustment. Therefore, no matter the environment or situation, I would not live in pain and suffering.

A view of life with no specific purpose like mine may very likely be misunderstood by the masses as passive and escapist. It is true that if one misused such views, it could really become passivity. Fortunately, I had faith in the Dharma, and I often reminded myself to have bodhi-mind as my basis, and use the Four Great Vows as my guidance. Although I didn't have my small personal goals, under any circumstances I would not lose sight of the greater direction and greater purpose for all sentient beings.

I Had Only One Identity

At present I play many roles, especially given that not only do I have to undertake different jobs at different times, I also have to do many types of jobs at the same time. At the time I was doing education and administration, I was also doing academic research, teaching Chan, leading Chan practices, writing Chan related books, and doing social service works for educating society.

In the aspect of my educational works on the development of the Chung-Hwa Institute of Buddhist Studies, we were gradually enhancing our team of faculty and researchers year by year, and also establishing cooperative relationships at the international level. Initially, our Institute of Buddhist Studies only had two full-time staff—one secretary and one professor. Currently, we already have ten or more professional staff, and besides the librarians and academic administration staffs, we have nine full-time professors and associate professors. The reason was that it was our plan to expand our Institute into a humanities and social community college, and proposed our application to the Ministry of Education.

In terms of academic activities, besides publishing the yearly issue of the *Chung-Hwa Buddhist Journal*, I also wrote theses and invited domestic and international Buddhist specialists to present theses on Buddhism. From 1989 on, the Chung-Hwa Institute of Buddhist Studies held a biennial Chung-Hwa International Conference on Buddhism. In the first conference, we invited over 50 Asian and western scholars from eighteen countries worldwide, organizing the conference by language into Chinese, English, and Japanese, and held in three separate auditoriums. The conference lasted three days and 40 theses were presented. Its theme was "From Tradition to Modernity" with a subtitle of "Buddhist Ethics and the Modern Society."

The conference venue was provided free of charge by the National Central Library, and the co-sponsors included the domestic Institute of Philosophy of National Taiwan University, the Philosophy Department of Soochow University, the Institute of Religious Studies of Fu Jen University, and the international Institute of Buddhist Culture of Bukkyo University of Kyoto, Japan; also, the Department of Religion of Temple University in America and the Department of Religion of the University of Hawaii. After the conference, Prof. Fu Weixun of the Department of Religion of Temple University and Prof. Sandra Wawrytko of the Department of Philosophy of San Diego University assisted in compiling both the Chinese and English versions of all the theses. The papers were forwarded to the Dongda Publishing Corp. in Taipei, Taiwan and the Greenwood Press in America respectively for publishing simultaneously.

The Chinese section included 15 theses, and the English section included 29 theses. Many of the theses were written in both Chinese and English, and published at the same time. For example, the two theses of mine concerning the precepts of the Late Ming Dynasty in China were such a case. The title for the English theses collection was *Buddhist Ethics and Modern Society*, and it received many very positive book reviews.

The Second Chung-Hwa International Conference on Buddhism happened this year from July 18 to 21 in 1992; it took three days and was held at the Grand Hotel in Taipei. We invited 35 scholars from more than ten countries worldwide. It was also conducted in three languages, and 26 theses were presented. The co-sponsors this time were all international universities and groups that had already established cooperative relationships with the Chung-Hwa Institute of Buddhist Studies and had engaged in academic, cultural collaboration and exchange of teachers and students. They included the Department of Buddhism of Rissho University in Tokyo, the Bukkyo University in Kyoto, the Institute of Religion of the University of Hawaii, the Institute of Buddhism of Michigan University in America, and the Dhammakaya Foundation in Thailand.

The domestic sponsors included the Council for Cultural Affairs of the Executive Yuan, Pacific Cultural Foundation Art Center, and the Ministry of Education of the Executive Yuan. The theme of this conference was still "Tradition to Modernity," and its subtitle was "Traditional Precepts and the Modern World." Other than delivering the opening and closing speech for the conference, and the keynote speech, I also published a thesis of over 20,000 words: *On the Bodhisattva Precept's Adaptation to Time and Space from the Perspective of Three Cumulative Pure Precepts.* After the meeting, the theses were also compiled into books by Prof. Fu Weixun and Prof. Sandra Wawrytko, and forwarded to the Greenwood Press in America for publishing.

As for the purpose of holding the International Conference on Buddhism, I mentioned in "The Cause for the Conference" on the first conference that was: "To be fully established in the Chinese Buddhist tradition, but to have a global vision for Buddhism as a whole; to introduce world Buddhism to China, and to spread Chinese Buddhism to the world." We were currently eagerly hoping to bring in the international Buddhist academic results, and hoping that the international Buddhist academic community would know that we were heading towards this direction too. We allowed them to provide us the experience and information, and at the same time allowed the domestic people inside and outside the Buddhist community to quickly recognize the importance and necessities of Buddhist academic research. We would then work together in nurturing the domestic talents.

In the opening speech at the Second Conference, I said: "A great religion should have three requirements: first, the practice of faith; second, a philosophical basis; and third, scholarship. If it does not have the practice of faith, then it will not be a religion, just ethical theory. The practice of faith of the religion must be grounded in deep philosophy as the basis for guidance, so that it would not degenerate into localized folk custom and irrational belief in ghosts and deities. Finally, if the religion did not conduct scholarly inquiry, then it would not know how to utilize the existing resources to provide the society with services in multiple functions and of high quality.

Buddhism has a profound philosophy as its basis, with simple and easy instructions on how to practice it. Therefore, besides putting my efforts into education and scholarship, I also taught Buddhism to ordinary people and did what I could to popularize it. I wrote three books in a tone that was easy to understand: (1) *Orthodox Chinese Buddhism*, completed in 1964, (2) *Buddhism: Some Basic Facts* (Chn. *Xuefo zhijin*), compiled in 1985, (3) *Questions and Answers on Buddhism* (Chn. *Xuefo qunyi*), completed in 1988. The distribution and scope of these books were very wide and some people referred to them as my "books of sermons."

In terms of popular lectures, I also gave many of them in Taiwan and Hong Kong in recent years, and every lecture was attended by an audience of at least a thousand up to six thousands. The lectures were also recorded into audiocassettes and were distributed in large quantities in Mandarin, Hokkien, and Cantonese.

The Chan methods I taught in the East and in the West were also very well received. In America since 1976, over three thousand students had learned sitting meditation from me directly and indirectly. In Taiwan, the people numbered over 30,000, and especially this year, we also attracted the high level professionals in society, including the executives from the various areas such as political, academic, business, arts and education, etc. The people who came to receive my Chan teachings grew gradually everyday and with good results.

I didn't leave out work in social care. Up to the spring of 1991, the Chung-Hwa Institute of Buddhist Culture and the Nung Chan Monastery gave winter relief and consolation for the poor, the total amount of relief provided last year amounting to $5,000,000 Taiwanese dollars. At the same time, we cooperated with the Huizhong (Benefit the People) Foundation of the Veterans General Hospital, and provided support for the patients who could not afford the medical expense, and must stay at the hospital for emergency rescue and medication. Learning the methods of a non-profit organization called Teacher Zhang and the Life Line organizations, we established a service called Door of Nectar at Nung Chan Monastery and the Veterans General Hospital to help ordinary people solve their problems and difficulties regarding their body and mind, family, career, etc.

We combined the various resources and the efforts of the monastic and lay disciples as well as the kind-hearted people to promote various social educational services and religious education. Over more than ten years, I received praise from the Ministry of the Interior and the Taipei City Government, and in 1991, I was elected as representative of the National Good People Good Deeds Award and was given the Eight Virtues Award. In 1992, I was selected by the Taipei City Government from the list of 75 recommended candidates, and chosen as one of the 25 awardees, and received the Civilian Honor Medal.

It was not my original intentions that led to such situations; what pushed me onto this road were the causes and conditions in reality. Therefore, what kind of a person I was at the present was not even clear to myself. Those who praised me would say that I was a Buddhist scholar and educator; some would say that I was a hard practicing religious leader, and some would say that I was a devoted social scholar who worked for the purification of society. Those who stood on the opposite position would look at me as someone who didn't focus on a certain specified role, so it may appear that I was doing everything, but actually not doing well in anything: "Doing a bit of everything but not standing firm on anything."

I believe these comments were all correct. My position was the attitude I have when teaching the methods of practice: how to deal with the many wandering thoughts that continuously float in one's mind when meditating. It should be like a person standing at the crossroads, looking at the cars, pedestrians, scenery, comings and goings, yet remaining silent, standing firm, unmoved by what was happening on the streets. The crowds of people and cars come and go in waves one after another, all of which we're fully aware of, but we would not be moved by the sounds and sights.

One should not be influenced by any one or certain scenes, nor leave one's original standpoint without noticing; nor should one just follow the crowds. That would be the best method for practice. At the time, even if there were wandering thoughts, one would still be practicing. Similarly, although I had many functions, I only had one purpose and direction, so I only had one identity and that would be a Buddhist monk.

My Central Thought

If one looked at the scope and characteristics of my studies and writings, they may appear to be huge and complex. Actually, at the stage when I was studying the *Tripitaka* in southern Taiwan, I already had a clear sequence of thoughts. I had to admit that Master Taixu and Master Yinshun had profound influence on me. When I was in Japan and writing the thesis, Master Ouyi influenced me. I mentioned before that Master Ouyi and Master Taixu both proposed the Great Harmony of the unified and integrated Buddhadharma, and it was the original characteristic that Chinese Buddhism stands firmly on.

Being Chinese I had feelings towards Chinese Buddhism, so not only could I understand its intentions, I also much admired its intentions. Chinese Buddhism should have the characteristics of Chinese culture. As for Master Yinshun, he stood at the basis of historical Buddhism in India to look at the development of Buddhism. Therefore, he did not become partial to Chinese Buddhism just because he was Chinese. The Buddhist thoughts of Master Yinshun originated from the *Agamas* and *Middle Treatise* (*Skt. Madhyamaka Shastra*), which meant that his standpoint was "Dependent Origination and the Nature of Emptiness." He then broadly studied Mahayana and Hinayana Buddhism in India as well as the thoughts of various schools in Chinese Buddhism.

In terms of my practice, I adopted the spirit of the original Buddhism which emphasized equal importance between the precepts, samadhi, and wisdom. Therefore, when I began the more comprehensive and in-depth research on Buddhist studies, I started with the issues of the precepts, then I studied various texts and sutras on the Chan studies, from the progressive methods of meditation practice in India to the sudden approach to enlightenment of the

Chinese Chan school. Actually, the *Agamas* in and of themselves teach wisdom along with samadhi. The studies of samadhi must be based on the precepts and guided by wisdom; otherwise, one either falls into the demonic states or stops at the worldly samadhis and is not able to gain liberation.

In terms of the studies on wisdom, I started with the original sutras of Indian Buddhism, the *Agamas*. I had very deep impressions on the concepts of the conditions of arising and perishing of what the *Agamas* taught as: "This arises, thus that arises; when this perishes then that perishes." Therefore, when I explained or described the basic principles of the Dharma, I would always start from and return to this standpoint. Regarding the Chan studies I was currently teaching, if one looked at the texts left by the masters of the Chinese Chan school, they belonged to the thoughts of the Tathagatagarbha system. However, I returned the Buddhadharma to the original point of dependent origination and the nature of emptiness. Whether I was guiding the methods of practice or teaching and clarifying the concepts of practice, I would always point out the fundamental position, which was the so-called Three Dharma Seals: impermanence, non-self, nirvana. If one deviated from the principles of the Three Dharma Seals, then it would easily be mixed up and mistaken for the notions of permanence or nihilism of the non-Buddhists.

As for my academic major, I devoted more time and put more mind into two items: First, I researched the Mahayana and Hinayana precepts. My first comparatively academic work was *The Essentials of Buddhist Sila and Vinaya*. In the First and the Second Chung-Hwa International Conferences on Buddhism, the theses I presented were also within this scope of research on precepts. Since *The Essentials of Buddhist Sila and Vinaya* was published in 1965, I continued to write works related to the precepts. There were 16 articles collected in the *Instructions on Learning Buddhism*, and eight articles were collected in the *Buddhist Living and Guidelines*. My purpose was not to be bound to the ancient and revive it, but to honor and adapt it to the practicality of the present time.

For example, I discovered that the three refuges and five precepts from the era of Shakyamuni Buddha were the common and correct concepts and living standards that all the lay followers would abide by, and yet coming to China, the five precepts became rules that were difficult to follow. Furthermore, the ten precepts of the shramanera and the eight precepts should be easy to keep, but in China they became something very difficult. Also, the bhikshu and bhikshuni precepts in India at the Buddha's time were not so strict that they could not be followed. However, in China, it seemed as if not many monks and nuns could keep the precepts in purity. The bodhisattva precepts had great flexibility, but in China, the precepts were muddled and confused by the different requirements from different bodhisattva precept sutras. If one could grasp the principles and spirits of upholding the Mahayana and Hinayana precepts, then it would not be difficult to apply them to the life of modern people. This was my motive in researching and writing on the precepts.

The second item I devoted most of my time to was related to the theme of my doctoral thesis, and that was Chinese Buddhism in late Ming Dynasty. Regarding the research on specific individuals as well as the specific research items, they were both historical and philosophical. The more advanced Japanese and Western scholars did a lot of research on Chinese Buddhism with the modernized method of studies, but they mostly set their eyes on the resource materials from ancient China. Very few people did research on the more recent Ming and Qing Buddhism and modern Buddhism in the 20th century. Actually, in the stage of the late Ming and early Qing dynasties, there were many master-grade lay and monastic scholars in the Buddhist community and they had influence on the development and continuation of modern Chinese Buddhism.

From the traditional position looking at modern Chinese Buddhism, whether it was the application studies or the studies of theories, including the thoughts of Chan, Precepts, Pure Land, Tiantai, Huayan, one could more or less find some information from the Buddhist thoughts from the late Ming. However, as I said in the Preface of *A Study of Buddhism During the Late Ming Dynasty*, "Before my academic thesis was published, the late Ming Buddhism was like a virgin land waiting to be developed by the academic community." Currently, although in America and domestically, several scholars have placed their emphasis of research on the Ming and Qing Buddhism, the material resources of Ming and Qing were very abundant, and there were still many areas to be researched. I was only "casting bricks to attract jade" (humbly disclosing one's thought to elicit more discussion and in-depth research from others).

In terms of research on religious studies, it was my interest between the ages 25 to 37. After 1968, I put it down. As for the Chan studies, I didn't do much academic research, though I was invited by Prof. Kenneth Kraft of Harvard University, and wrote a thesis titled *Sitting Meditation* for his compiled book, *Zen: Tradition and Transition*. It was a discussion on the changes in sitting meditation from the historical point of view, and was published by the Grove Press in 1988. I also wrote "Chan and the Chan School," "Thoughts of the Platform Sutra," which were published in the *Chung-Hwa Buddhist Journal*. Nevertheless, I was not an expert on researching the topics of Chan studies, and I was only using the Chan material resources to spread the practice of Chan.

Although I had published over ten books related to Chan in both Chinese and English, they were actually practical guides on the concepts and methods. I also published "Research on Tantric Buddhism" and "Research on the Thoughts of Pure Land," and during the period I studied abroad, I wrote articles such as "The Tiantai Thought of Three Thousand Worlds Immanent in an Instant of One Thought." Recently, I also paid attention to the Buddhist thoughts of Prasangika Madhyamaka of Tibetan Buddhism. In the autumn of 1992, I published a book *A Dialogue on the Similarities and Differences in Chinese and Tibetan Buddhism* (Chn. *Hanzang foxue tongyi wenda*), and it was just my sideline, not my expertise.

In terms of my overall thought, I did not belong to any school or sect, but when I explained a certain sutra, shastra, or works written by the Chinese ancestral masters, I would not use the standpoints of original Buddhism to explain them. I would say what was written in the texts and I would use their own thoughts to introduce their thoughts. For example, when I taught the Five Essential Teachings of Huayan, I wouldn't use the viewpoints of the *Agamas* or *Middle Treatise* (*Skt. Madhyamaka Shastra*) to comment on it. When I taught the *Awakening of Mahayana Faith*, and *The Sutra of Complete Enlightenment*, I would not use the viewpoints of the Consciousness-Only school to explain them. When I taught the *Treatise on the Doctrine of Consciousness-Only*, I would not mix it with the Tathagatagarbha thoughts.

Up to the present, I do not belong to any school nor must I say that I was a Chan master or master of a certain school. If one would clarify the source of the Buddhadharma and return to the fundamental thoughts of the Buddha's era, then one could merge oneself with Buddhism in its entirety. One could understand, sympathize, and recognize the Buddhist thoughts of various schools and sects, and would neither be influenced by the differences between them nor hold the notion that only one's own thoughts were correct. I should say that I was like a person standing at the crossroad watching the beautiful scenery on the streets, and that would be my central thought.

This small book should come to an end at this point. I should thank the chief editor Prof. Fu Weixun for compiling this set of *The Study and Thought of Contemporary Academics*, and providing me the chance to write this book. I also thank Cheng Chung Books for accepting this book of mine.

Chan Meditation Center
Elmhurst, New York
December 19, 1992

The Chronicle

1930 Born in Jiangsu Province, China.

1943 Becomes a novice at Guangjiao Monastery, Nantong, Jiangsu province.

1949 Joins the army and arrives in Taiwan from Shanghai during Chinese Civil War.

1959 Ends his 10-year service in the army, and is re-ordained by Venerable Master Dongchu.

1961 Begins his six-year solitary retreat at Chaoyuan Monastery in Kaohsiung.

1969 Begins his studies at Rissho University in Tokyo, Japan and earns doctorate in Buddhist Literature in 1975.

1975 Heads to the States to spread the Dharma.

1977 Returns to Taiwan taking over the reins of Chung-Hwa Institute of Buddhist Culture and Nung Chan Monastery by Ven. Master Dongchu's will.

1978 Receives Dharma transmission of the Linji lineage from Venerable Master Lingyuan.

1979 Establishes a monastery in New York named Chan Meditation Center.

1980 Ordains first group of disciples in Taiwan, marking the beginning of the DDM Sangha.

1985 Establishes the Chung-Hwa Institute of Buddhist Studies in Beitou, Taipei.

1989 Establishes Dharma Drum Mountain.

1992 Proposes Protecting the Spiritual Environment as the core DDM vision.

1997 Sets up the Dharma Drum Retreat Center in Pine Bush, New York. Attends the 11th International Meeting People and

Religions in Padua, Italy and meets with Pope John Paul II at the Vatican.

1998 Holds a dialogue with the Dalai Lama in New York City, titled "In the Spirit of Manjushri: The Wisdom Teachings of Buddhism".

1999 Proposes the Fivefold Spiritual Renaissance Campaign: A lifestyle for the 21st century.

2000 Attends and makes a keynote speech at the Millennium World Peace Summit of Religious and Spiritual Leaders held at the UN headquarters in New York.

2001 Establishes the Dharma Drum Sangha University in Taiwan.

2002 Attends the World Economic Forum in New York as a Buddhist leader, donates and escorts the Akshobhya Buddha head statue, stolen in 1997, back to Four Gate Pagoda in Shandong province, China.

2003 Makes a speech at the meeting for the World Council of Religious Leaders at the UN headquarters in NY at the invitation of the UN secretary Kofi Annan. Travels to Israel and Palestine with representative leaders from WCRL for religious peace movement.

2004 Attends the Seminar on Preventing Terrorism held by WCRL in New York.

2005 Attends Leaders' Meeting on Faith and Development organized by the World Bank in Dublin, Ireland. Receives honorary doctorate degree from Mahachulalongkorn-rajavidyalaya Buddhist University, Thailand. Inauguration for the DDM World Center for Buddhist Education takes place.

2006 Leads a delegation of 15 DDM youth leaders to attend the UN Global Youth Leadership Summit at the UN headquarters in New York.

2007 Establishes Dharma Drum Buddhist College in Taiwan established the Sheng Yen Professorship in Chinese Buddhism at Columbia University, New York. Initiates the Six Ethics of the Mind campaign. The Taipei County Jinshan Eco-friendly Memorial Garden starts operation.

2009 Passes away on February 3rd. Receives posthumous honors from the President of R.O.C.

Also by Chan Master Sheng Yen

AUTOBIOGRAPHY
Footprints in the Snow

CHAN PRACTICE
Attaining the Way
A guide to the practice of Chan Buddhism

Chan Comes West

Getting The Buddha Mind
On the practice of Chan retreat

Hoofprint of the Ox
Principles of the Chan buddhist path as taught by a modern Chinese master

Illuminating Silence
The practice of Chinese Zen (Silent Illumination)

In the Spirit of Ch'an
An introduction to Chan Buddhism

Ox Herding at Morgan's Bay

Shattering the Great Doubt
The Chan practice of Huatou

Subtle Wisdom
Understanding suffering, cultivating compassion through Chan Buddhism

The Method of No-Method
The Chan practice of Silent Illumination

The Poetry of Enlightenment
Poems by ancient Chan masters

CHAN MASTER'S DISCOURSE
Faith in Mind
A commentary on Seng Ts'an's classic

Song of Mind
Wisdom from the Zen classic Xin Ming

The Infinite Mirror
Commentaries on two Chan classics

The Sword of Wisdom
A commentary on the Song of Enlightenment

DHARMA FOR DAILY LIFE
Dharma Drum
The life & heart of Chan practice

Zen Wisdom
Conversations on Buddhism

BUDDHADHARMA
Orthodox Chinese Buddhism

Setting in Motion the Dharma Wheel

The Six Paramitas
Perfections of the Budhisattva path, a commentary

Things Pertaining to Bodhi
The thirty-seven aids to enlightenment

SUTRA COMMENTARIES
There is No Suffering:
A commentary on the Heart Sutra

Complete Enlightenment - Zen Comments on the Sutra of Complete Enlightenment

For more of Master Sheng Yen's teachings, please visit the website:
www.shengyen.org

What I am unable to accomplish in this lifetime,

I vow to push forward through countless future lives;

what I am unable to accomplish personally,

I appeal to everyone to undertake together.

— Master Sheng Yen (1930-2009)